86 CUB SCOUT annual

The Official Cub Scout Annual of the Scout Association
Edited by David Harwood

Contents

World
Published in Great Britain
by World International Publishing Limited.
P. O. Box 111, Great Ducie Street, MANCHESTER M60 3BL.
Printed in Great Britain.
SBN 7235 6742 5

A CUB FOR ALL SEASONS: SPRING

Isn't Spring a wonderful time of the year? The buds on the trees are beginning burst, and the grey and brown landscape of Winter is transformed as if by mag into a beautiful patchwork of colour. Hibernating animals like the hedgehog a the squirrel wake up from their Winter sleep, and even Cub Scouts feel the ur to get out and about!

As Winter draws to a close, go out and look for signs of Spring. This happy Cub could hardly miss the magnificent display of Spring flowers on this bush! Earlier in the season, you can look for the first snowdrops, and the tips of the daffodils pushing up through the soil. Look also at the buds on the trees: most begin to swell quite early on, and it is very exciting to observe trees and shrubs to see how they develop day by day during the Spring.

Many Cub Scouts take part in Scout Job Week to raise money for Scouting, and this always takes place at Eastertime. This lucky Cub has managed to get the job of cleaning a fire appliance at his local fire station! Other Cubs have done such things as washing elephants to earn **their** money! If your Pack takes part in Scout Job Week, why not try and get yourself an unusual job? If you do, write and tell us about it . . . you might then find yourself in the **Cub Scout Annual**!

St. George is the Patron Saint of Scouts, and every year around 23rd April (which is St. George's Day), Cubs and Scouts all over the country hold parades and church services. Here a Scout Group — complete with band — is on parade. Maybe your Group has a band, but even if it doesn't, you can still make sure you are smart whenever you go on parade!

Spring is the time to get out into the countryside, and what better way than to go on a Pack ramble? These Cubs are on a day out at Dovedale which is a beautiful part of the valley of the River Dove in Derbyshire.

written by Gill Pawley

1986 marks the 70th Anniversary of the start of Cub Scouting, and over the past 70 years Cubs have got up to all kinds of things! In the next few pages you will see and read about just a few of the things which have happened.

How it all began . . .

Many people know about the camp which Robert Baden-Powell held in 1907 for 20 boys on Brownsea Island near Poole in Dorset which marked the start of Scouting. But what about Cubs? How did they start? Well, many of those who became Boy Scouts had younger brothers who also wanted to get involved. They kept asking if **they** could join the Scouts, and they were so determined that, in 1916, B.-P. officially started the Wolf Cub Section.

One of B.-P.'s great friends was Rudyard Kipling who had written *The Jungle Book*. B.-P. liked many of the ideas in it, and based some of the training programme and organisation on the stories and the characters in *The Jungle Book*. The new 'junior' Scouts were called 'Wolf Cubs' and met in Packs, just like the wolves in the book. Pack Leaders were known as 'Akela' (after the Great Grey Lone Wolf), and other Scouters took their names from the other jungle animals; so that's much the same as today, too.

When Wolf Cubs began, the First World War was being fought in Europe and many men were away fighting. In lots of places, the Leaders of the Wolf Cub Packs were women. As Britain was at war, lots of things were in short supply and many families had to save up for the uniform of a green jersey, a green cap with yellow piping and the scarf. Despite the shortages, the boys did lots of different activities and had a great time.

Badges and Tests

Just as you have Arrows and Proficiency Badges, so Wolf Cubs worked for their badges.

First of all, a boy had to pass the Tenderpad Test before he could be invested as a Wolf Cub. He had to know, among other things, about the Grand Howl, the Wolf Cub Salute, and the Wolf Cub Promise and Law. These were slightly changed a few years ago, but not really very much.

1916
Wolf Cubs from the 16th North Poplar Pack in London doing the Grand howl.

The Grand Howl contained some strange sounding "DYBs" and "DOBs"! This is how it went:

Akela: Pack! Pack! Pack!
Cubs: Pack! (*Then they formed a circle*) Akela! We'll do our BEST!
Sixer: DYB — DYB — DYB!
Cubs: We'll DOB — DOB — DOB!

DYB stood for "Do Your Best!", and DOB meant "Do Our Best". So, as you can see, it isn't really very different from the Grand Howl which you do today.

The difference in the Salute is the number of fingers used. Wolf Cubs made the salute with two fingers representing the two alert ears of the wolf, whereas the Salute you use now with three fingers represents the three parts of your Cub Scout Promise.

The Law of the Wolf Cub Pack was:

1. The Cub gives in to the Old Wolf;
2. The Cub does not give into himself.

The Wolf Cub's Promise was:

I promise to DO MY BEST

1. To be loyal to God, the King and the Law of the Wolf Cub Pack,
2. And to do a good turn to somebody every day.

Once they were invested, Wolf Cubs worked for two Stars, worn on their caps. The 'tests' for the Stars were similar to those for the Bronze, Silver and Gold Arrows of today.

Great Occasions

Once the Wolf Cub Section had been established, it became clear that thousands of boys were enjoying their Cubbing. In fact, in the early years, every time there was a big gathering of Scouts, Wolf Cubs were there as well!

You may have heard that the World Scout Jamboree was held in Canada in 1983, or that the next World Scout Jamboree will be in Australia in 1987. The very first World Jamboree was held at Olympia in London in 1920 . . . and 500 Wolf Cubs were there, too!

In 1922 there was a Rally at Alexandra Palace, again in London. The Prince of Wales of that time went to see what was going on . . . and he found 20,000 Wolf Cubs.

In 1924, the Prince of Wales' brother (the Duke of York, who would later become King George VI) was the Guest of Honour at the Empire Jamboree at Wembley in London. There was a special Cub Day when many, many Cubs performed the Dance of Kaa.

1916
Boys from the 11th East Ham in London practise signalling by semaphore.

(left)
1926
A group of boys from Nottingham photographed with their Leaders. Note that the scarves are tied and that some of the boys have gained their First or Second Stars which are worn in their caps.

(above left)

1938
Boys showing Pack Leaders how the Investiture Ceremony is performed at a Conference at the Scouters' Training Centre, Gilwell Park, Chingford. You can see the Wolf Cubs' Salute, and how long their shorts were.

(above right)

1948
An Akela with two of her Wolf Cubs earning some money during Bob-a-Job Week. (A bob was the popular description of a shilling which is worth 5p today.)

1954
Some more Wolf Cubs at work during Bob-a-Job Week . . . who's taking whom for a walk?

1968
Cub Scouts enjoying a day out at camp.

Worldwide Scouts

As a Cub Scout you are a member of the worldwide brotherhood of Scouts — and today there are more than 15 million Scouts throughout the world. Soon after Scouts started in the United Kingdom, the Scout Movement spread to other countries. In 1908 (the same year in which Scouting was established in the United Kingdom) Scouts got under way in Australia, Belgium, Gibraltar, Ireland, Malta, New Zealand and South Africa. From then on, it spread round the world like wildfire.

A new name for Cubs

You may have been wondering when and why 'Wolf Cubs' were changed to 'Cub Scouts' in the United Kingdom. As Scouting approached its 60th Birthday, it was decided to make some changes. Sir Charles Maclean, the Chief Scout at the time, inspired many of these alterations. Training programmes were brought up to date, the names of the Sections changed from Wolf Cubs, Boy Scouts, Senior Scouts and Rover Scouts to Cub Scouts, Scouts and Venture Scouts. There were new uniforms, too, which particularly affected Scouts. For more than 60 years, Boy Scouts had worn large, broad-brimmed hats and shorts as

part of their uniform. Now these were replaced by long trousers and berets which you will wear when you join the Scouts.

Today

After all this time, what are Cubs doing today?

Whenever The Scout Association has staged a national or an international event, Cubs have been there. But, in recent years, there have been a number of events just for Cubs.

One of the largest recent events was **Cub Country** in 1979. 1979 was the International Year of the Child, and Cubs raised £165,000 for Scouts in Nepal, which is a small country at the foot of the Himalayas. It's a beautiful part of the world but is very poor, with many remote villages in the hills.

Cub Country was a three year project during which UK Cub Scouts raised money so that the Scouts of Nepal could buy seeds to distribute to local vegetable growers in many villages.

The Cubs who took part learnt about the problems of living in that kind of terrain, as well as the particular problems of its people.

A few years ago, Cubs went wild making cups of tea! In 1982 and 1983 the Tea Council held a National Tea-Making Fortnight. In 1982, 5,000 Cub Scout Packs took part, and there were 1,000 more in 1983. The boys made and drank tea all over the place . . . down coal mines, in police stations, on buses, down cellars, with animals at zoos . . .

1981
Cub Scouts Andy Davison and Chris Kimber meet Major-General Michael Walsh who became the new Chief Scout in 1982; behind them is the statue of Lord Baden-Powell without whose enthusiasm and imagination there would have been no Scouting . . .

1977
Scouting's 70th Birthday!
A fanfare from three Cub Scout buglers.

Cubs of the Future

Cub Scouts of 1986 might do different things from the Wolf Cubs of 1916, just as Cubs in 2006 will be doing different things again. We might even have the first Cub Scout astronaut by then! But one thing is certain — boys of today will enjoy being in Cubs as much as the early ones, and that goes for all Cubs everywhere, now and in the future.

So, Happy Birthday, Cub Scouts . . . and may you, and those who come after you in the years ahead, have many, many Happy Returns!

This sort of picture could have been taken at almost any time in Scouting's history — a boy having fun . . .

Animal Homes

written and illustrated by Stephen Roberts

'Home' to an animal may be any place where it can find rest, shelter or safety, protecting it from its enemies and providing it with a refuge where it can breed and raise its young. Some creatures have no permanent home, some make use of whatever is available and others make extremely elaborate structures.

Studying animal homes is fascinating, and finding out why different animals make different sorts of homes is very interesting. Here we give you just a few examples. See how many more you can discover for yourself.

Weaver bird

Tailor bird

Harvest mouse

Oven bird

The weaver bird suspends its nest from the ends of slender branches with the entrance at the bottom to protect it from marauding snakes.

The tailor bird actually sews two leaves together with either cotton fibres or cobwebs or silk from cocoons. The thread is taken through holes which have been pierced in the leaves with its beak.

The oven bird lays its eggs within the hollow chamber of a baked mud structure.

The harvest mouse builds a nest supported by a framework of corn stalks. This home has no entrance as such as the occupants burrow in and out.

Trapdoor spider

Prairie dogs

The badger

The burrowing owl

The spotted flycatcher

Blue tit

A young orangutan

Hermit crab

Wood ants' nest

A hornets' nest

A termite mound

Many creatures excavate underground homes or burrows. The **badgers**' set is a well known example but did you know that such creatures as **hyenas**, **prairie dogs** and **burrowing owls** also make burrows?

The **trapdoor spider** has a 'front door' to his home behind which he hides, ready to pounce on unsuspecting prey.

Some birds will make their homes almost anywhere! For example, the **spotted flycatcher** will set up house in anything from an old kettle to a baked bean can! **Blue tits** are among those birds which regularly use nest boxes.

Home for a **hermit crab** is any shell that will contain its growing body, for as it gets larger so it leaves one shell and looks for a bigger one. The young **orangutan** has no permanent home and is shown sheltering under a leaf.

Insects find safety in numbers. Hundreds of thousands of **wood ants** live in mounds made from earth and wood chips. Over a million **termites** may live inside a termite mound, which can stand up to ten metres high and provides a warm, safe environment for its inhabitants. Colonies of **hornets** work together to build nests of wood pulp; sometimes they use man-made materials like paper as well.

One of the master builders must be the **beaver**. It dams rivers and streams to create ideal conditions to build its lodge. Sometimes it is a huge affair with its entrances below the level of the water.

A beaver lodge

CUB SCOUT PUZZLE PAGE

TOPS AND TAILS *CAN YOU WORK OUT THE NAMES OF THE EIGHT PROFICIENCY BADGES BELOW BY LOOKING AT THE PICTURES AND CHANGING SOME OF THE LETTERS?*

NINE PHOTOGRAPHS *HERE ARE NINE 'PHOTOGRAPHS' OF A CUB SCOUT TAKEN OVER A PERIOD OF TIME, BUT THEY ARE NOT IN THE CORRECT SEQUENCE. CAN YOU WORK OUT IN WHICH ORDER THEY WERE TAKEN?*

INITIAL LETTER JUMBLE *TAKE THE FIRST LETTER OF EACH OF THE SHAPES YOU CAN FIND IN THE JUMBLE BELOW – THEN TRY AND ARRANGE THESE LETTERS TO MAKE FOUR WORDS IN THE GRID AT THE BOTTOM. THE ANSWER IS SOMETHING YOU SHOULD KNOW!*

ANSWERS ON PAGE 63

How to find the direction of TRUE NORTH

drawn by Malcolm Turner
devised by David Harwood and David Harrold

CHURCHES (ESPECIALLY ROMAN CATHOLIC AND CHURCH OF ENGLAND) CAN GIVE YOU THE BASIC COMPASS POINTS. THE ALTAR IS USUALLY AT THE EASTERN END, AND AS CHURCHES ARE OFTEN CROSS SHAPED, THE OTHER POINTS CAN BE WORKED OUT QUITE EASILY.

OF COURSE, IF THERE'S A WEATHER VANE ON TOP OF A CHURCH OR OTHER BUILDING, YOU HAVE A READY MADE WAY OF FINDING THE DIRECTION OF NORTH, SOUTH, EAST & WEST. BUT YOU MIGHT BE WISE TO CHECK, JUST IN CASE THE VANE HAS MOVED FROM ITS CORRECT POSITION!

ON A CLEAR NIGHT YOU CAN USE THE STARS IN THE SKY. IN THE NORTHERN HEMISPHERE THE POLE STAR CAN BE TAKEN AS TRUE NORTH. TO FIND THE POLE STAR, LOOK FOR THE GROUP OF SEVEN STARS CALLED 'THE PLOUGH' (THIS GROUP IS ALSO CALLED 'THE GREAT BEAR', 'THE BIG DIPPER' AND – ITS PROPER NAME – URSA MAJOR) OR THE GROUP CALLED CASSIOPEIA.

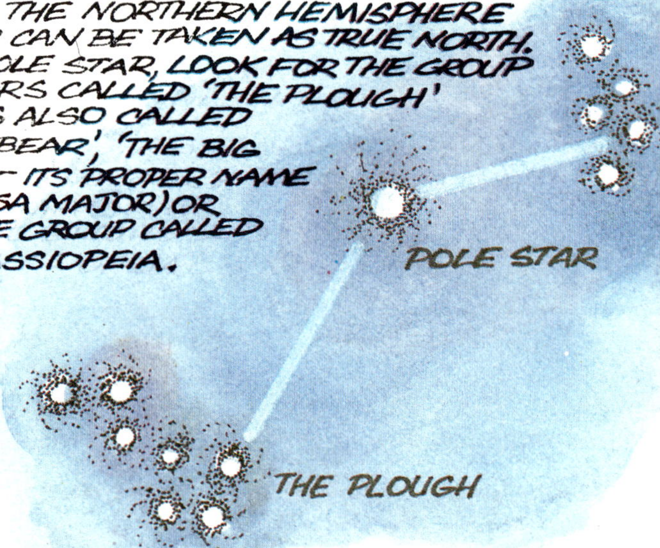

ON A SUNNY DAY, YOU CAN USE THE SUN AND A WATCH TO FIND THE APPROXIMATE DIRECTION OF NORTH & SOUTH. POINT THE HOUR HAND OF THE WATCH TO THE SUN – TRUE SOUTH WILL BE IN THE DIRECTION MIDWAY BETWEEN THE HOUR HAND AND '12' ON THE FACE OF THE WATCH.

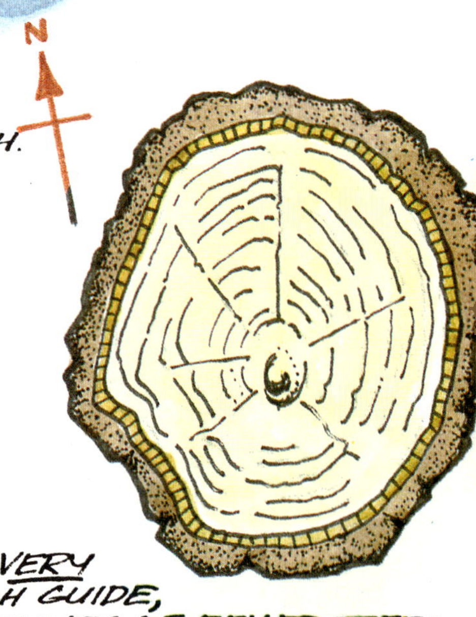

IF YOU STAND WITH THE SUN DIRECTLY IN FRONT AT NOON G.M.T. YOU WILL BE FACING SOUTH – YOUR SHADOW WILL POINT IN THE DIRECTION OF NORTH.

AS A VERY ROUGH GUIDE, THE STUMPS OF FELLED TREES SHOW AN ODD TENDENCY TO EXTRA THICKNESS ON THEIR NORTH & NORTH-EAST SIDES.

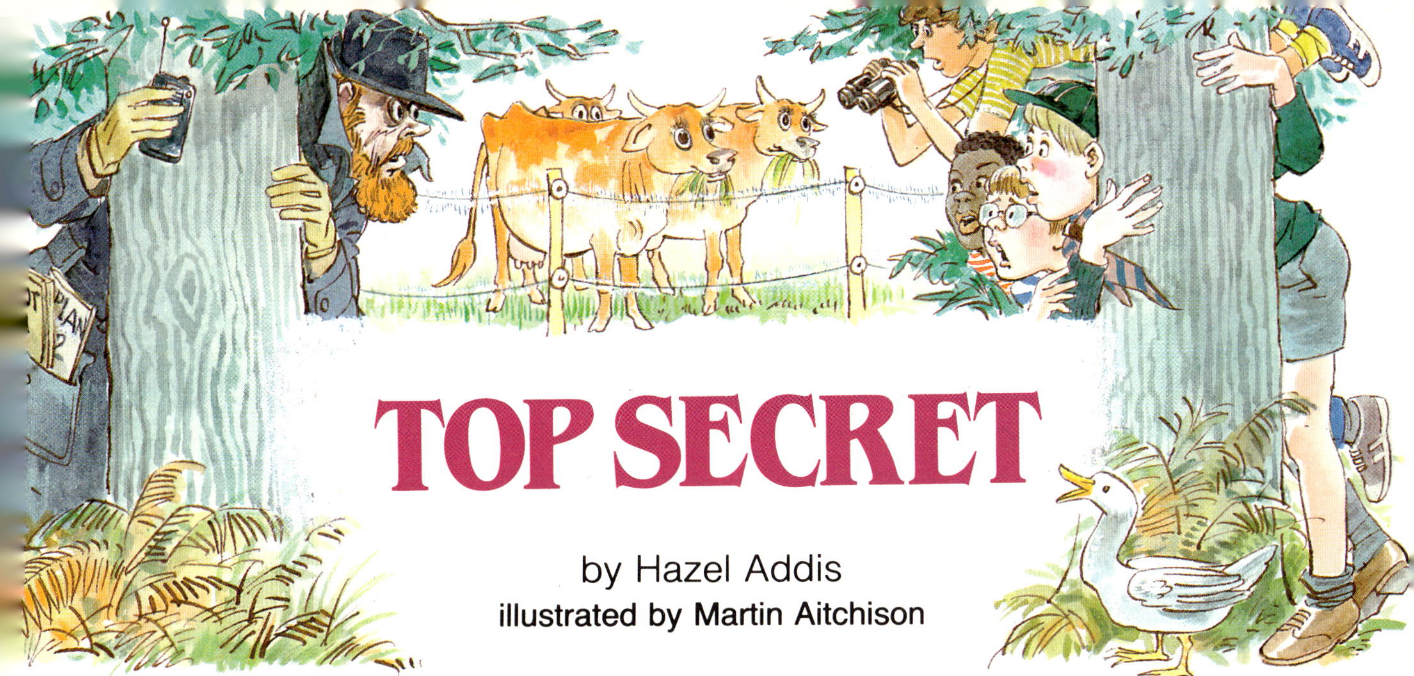

TOP SECRET

by Hazel Addis

illustrated by Martin Aitchison

"That," announced Akela, "is a Top Secret Ministry of Defence place."

"What for?"

"You don't ask questions about Top Secrets because no one's allowed to answer them. Our job is to defend it."

The Cubs glanced at Akela to make sure that he was looking at what they were looking at. He was. He was actually pointing to the fence that surrounded the grassy field.

"And are those special weapons?" asked Tim. "Disguised as cows?"

"Don't be stupid!" Ginger told him. "They're bulls disguised as cows."

The boys belonged to a Cub Scout Pack from a town somewhere in the Midlands where the landscape was houses and factories and roads and industrial buildings. They hadn't been to camp before so spending a few days on a farm sleeping in a large empty barn was a new experience for them. It was the first time they had seen this herd of animals because the barn and the rest of their camp was on the other side of the hill. They'd been busy learning about camping and the country and having fun.

Akela had told them that today was to be Adventure Day, while tomorrow had to be Tidy-Up Day because tomorrow afternoon the local Assistant District Commissioner for Cub Scouts, a Miss Walsh, would be coming to visit them and the pillow fight they'd had in the barn last night had left rather a lot of straw lying about . . .

This, then, was Adventure Day.

"Some adventure," Nick thought. "How could you have an adventure all to do with cows?" Then he grumbled out loud: "Give me tanks every time. They don't keep staring at you like that."

"Tanks don't give you milk, neither," said another.

"That lot can keep their milk and bust. I like mine out of a bottle."

"Suppose you shut up and listen?" Akela said, raising his voice. So they tried. "The Police have had a tip-off that a Secret Agent is trying to get in there today . . ."

"Maybe someone grassed on him!" Nick chuckled, looking at the cows making a meal of the field.

Akela gave Nick a black look.

"I've promised that we'll help," Akela con-

tinued. "Shall we?" Of course they would. "Well, wait until we've got a plan of campaign. The wire fence is electrified, so if you touch it, you're dead."

"So is the Agent!" a brainy one piped up.

"That's why he'll have to think up some special cunning way to get in. Anyone got any ideas?"

"What happens if a cow touches the wire?" asked Mike.

Several people answered, "Roast beef!" but Akela was being serious. "Try and work out a really clever means of defence."

"Alert the cows," suggested John. "They'd do the job much better than us."

"Why don't we disguise ourselves as cows?" suggested Andrew. "We'd be able to keep a really good look-out then." Everyone groaned. Andrew was full of good ideas, but most of them weren't very practicable.

"And where are we going to get about 18 cow costumes from?" asked Ginger. And that was the end of Andrew's suggestion.

"The cows will be going back to the farm for milking soon, so we'll have to hide ourselves until the Police arrive," Akela continued. "Any other ideas?" There weren't, so Akela outlined his plan: "I suggest the Yellow Six find the best place to keep a lookout — where they can see without being seen. OK, Tim?" The Yellow Sixer nodded. "If you can't find any natural cover, you may have to camouflage yourselves or build a hide. As you've got your Explorer Badge, Tim, you should know all about that. Now, Mark, the Black Six might scout round for the most likely place where the Agent might try to break in. The farmer knows what we're doing. Don't forget the electric wire."

"We're not daft!" replied Mark. Mark had gained his Gold Arrow, so Akela gave him a sketch map of the field, and asked him to fill in any landmarks and to put a big black cross at any place where he thought there might be danger.

"Hey! What about us?" asked John, the Red Sixer.

"All right! All right! I've not forgotten you lot. The Red Six can work out the communications — very important work — some sort of code in signs or sounds is needed, so that everyone can let everyone else know what's going on. Except, of course, the Agent — you mustn't give the game away to him. OK?"

The members of the Red Six were standing staring, rather like the cows.

"As you've got your Entertainer Badge, John, I'm sure you'll be able to produce this part of the show. Come back and tell me when you've got something worked out. I'll be up this tree."

"Disguised as a squirrel or something?" asked Mike.

"No, an owl. One hoot means that the Yellows should come back, two hoots for the Blacks, and three hoots for the Reds." Akela cupped his hands to his mouth and blew between his thumbs, producing a very realistic bell-like hoot. None of the Cubs could do it however hard they spluttered, but Akela said: "Don't practise now. Remember, half the success of this operation will be to keep QUIET. Off you go!"

Off they went, sounding more like three swarms of bees than the usual monkey-house racket. Akela climbed into a comfortable fork in his tree and settled down to watch out for Kim. Kim was a Venture Scout who was helping with the Pack as a Cub Scout Instructor. During lunch an hour before, he had made a point of asking Akela if he could go on a hike by himself for the afternoon. Of course, Akela had said yes. After the washing up had been done, the Cubs had waved Kim off as he strode down the lane away from the barn with a pack on his back. They didn't expect to see him again until early evening. They didn't see Akela give Kim a wink — nor did they notice Kim wink back.

From his branch up the tree Akela looked in all directions. There was no sign of Kim. He saw the Blacks trying to find out if a rabbit hole was really a tunnel burrowing under the fence. Mark had his head and shoulders in the hole for some time before he decided it wasn't spy-shaped. He had to be dragged out by the legs.

Quite soon the Reds were back, looking very pleased with themselves.

"We done it!" shouted John in a whisper. "Animal noises! Country noises!"

"A great idea!" Akela said enthusiastically, peering down from his perch. "How does it work?"

John had discovered that Mike could bark rather like a dog, and young Tony could do a duck. "One bark or one quack means we've seen him," John explained. "Two quacks or barks means we haven't. OK?"

"No it's not," said Akela, "because that would mean noises all the time, if you think about it. Why not do one quack or bark for we've seen him, like you said, and two quacks or barks for we need help! Right?"

"Right!" and John listened as Akela went on to suggest that two Reds went to each of the other Sixes — one as the signaller, and the other as a messenger in case of need.

"Mike can go and bark for the Yellows up there behind those bushes which keep bobbing and moving about. Quacker and his runner will find the Blacks hiding somewhere near that oak tree. See? John and Titch stay with me as I may need a noise interpreter."

The Reds scattered, while the Sixer and the smallest Cub climbed onto a branch below Akela.

"Look how all the cows are going away," whispered John.

"That's because they know it's milking time," explained Akela. "Which means it's spy or agent-time for us."

"Do you think . . ."

"Yes. But not out loud," said Akela quickly.

During the silence that followed, broken only by the hum of bees, Akela was still watching out for Kim. There was still no sign of him. Or was there?

Suddenly there was an uproar. A pack of dogs started barking somewhere up the hill and, almost at the same time, a flock of ducks broke into a chorus of quacks from the opposite direction.

John groaned. It was his code all right, but he hadn't realised that *everyone* would want to signal for himself all at the same time. The two Cubs and Akela jumped down from the tree to meet the Yellows who were charging down the hill, sheep-dogging a man with a beard. The man was heading towards them. Akela watched in disbelief as the man got closer. It looked as though he'd got a *grey* beard. Had Kim thought of sprinkling it with some flour?

The man put a hand over his beard, as though he was frightened it might be jerked off, but above that his eyes were twinkling. Akela looked and felt very embarrassed.

The man laughed loudly. "Don't worry!" he said.

"But who *are* you?" Akela asked.

The man laughed again. "I'm the farmer's brother. I sometimes come over to help him with the afternoon milking. He told me you were having an Adventure Day — but I didn't expect to be able to join in the fun! Looking for Agents, are you?" The boys' mouths dropped open and they stood gawping. So did Akela. "I used to be a Cub, you know," the man said. "I was a Scout, too." The cows were bellowing louder than ever. "Well, I'd better get back to my milking, if you've done with me. It sounds as though that lot have had better luck with a real Agent!"

Sure enough, the quacks had given way to shouting, and Ginger was beckoning frantically. "WE GOT 'IM!" he yelled. "And watcher think? *He's* dressed up as a woman — and a Scout-woman at that!"

Akela ran rather faster than usual. He found Miss Walsh, the Assistant District Commissioner for Cub Scouts, sitting quietly on a log with two members of the Black Six proudly standing guard behind her. Akela gave the guards a look which was blacker than a thundercloud. He began to apologise to Miss Walsh, while the ducks stood round with their beaks wide open.

"Don't worry!" chuckled the Commissioner. "It was great fun. I'm sorry that I've come a day earlier than I said. But I'm glad I did. I wouldn't have missed this for anything!"

They all went back to camp for tea which Rikki had been making while they were out. Rikki had even tidied up the straw in the barn, so everything looked all right. Then Akela realised that Kim was still missing. Where on earth was he?

While the boys were settling down to tuck into the sandwiches, cakes and squash, Miss Walsh explained that her car had had a puncture, which was why she'd left the road and walked up the path right into the Blacks' trap. "A funny thing happened," she went on. "I was just about to jack up the car to change the wheel when a very odd-looking man appeared from nowhere and offered to do it for me. He obviously knew what he was doing, so I left him to it."

"But he may steal your car!" exclaimed Titch.

"I don't think he was that sort, although I must admit he was eccentric. He had a red beard which seemed to slip a bit when he started working."

Some of the Cubs yelped with excitement . . . false beard, funny-looking and all . . . *he* must have been the Secret Agent!

"Have you seen anyone like that, Kim?" demanded John. Kim had returned almost unnoticed from the direction of the barn.

He slipped the pack off his back. "No, *I* didn't see anyone in the least suspicious," Kim replied.

The Pack all spoke at once, trying to tell him about all the fun he had missed. It sounded like the normal monkey house again. None of them saw him slip a set of small keys into Miss Walsh's hand when they shook hands after Akela had 'officially' introduced him to the Commissioner.

"Whatever have you been doing this afternoon, then?" Tim asked.

"Just Scouting," Kim replied.

"Like what?"

"Like Top Secret!"

Same Sound–Different Spelling

by Daphne Pitcher

This is a crossword with a difference. In each of the clues one of the words has not been spelt correctly. What you have to do is to identify that word and put its correct spelling in the answer grid.

Clues Across

1. Not the May Day fare
3. Not her waste size
5. Not the ruff road
6. It was piece and war
8. Do weight at the road
9. The shop is having a sail
10. Go and by the meat, please
11. Have you bean to Wembley?
12. I'm going to meat Bill
13. That is a grate big cake!
14. Some seaside towns have two peers
16. Stay their!
17. He was the soul survivor

Clues Down

1. Fur trees are evergreens
2. That sum is not write
4. It is rude to stair
6. In church you prey to God
7. He was ate on his last birthday
8. Ring out your swimming things — they're still too wet
9. You hope the son will shine when you're on holiday
10. You beet eggs to make omelettes
11. That's not an oak, it's a beach!
12. The men are repairing the manes in the road
15. Can you sea the signpost?

Solution on page 63

ITCH . . . CUB SCOUT

by Leslie Cecil

ANIMAL KINGDOM PUZZLE PAGE

HOW MANY INSECTS? *BUZZING ROUND OUR ANXIOUS CUB THERE ARE ALL SORTS OF INSECTS. HOW MANY CAN YOU FIND IN THE CIRCLE OF LETTERS, STARTING FROM THE YELLOW DOT AT THE TOP AND GOING IN A CLOCKWISE DIRECTION?*

THREE IN ONE *THERE ARE THREE ANIMALS IN THE SHAPES BELOW. TO FIND OUT WHAT THEY ARE, FILL IN THE SHAPES WITH A 'DOT' IN ONE COLOUR; THEN THE SHAPES WITH A 'CROSS' IN ANOTHER COLOUR; AND THE SHAPES WITH A 'CIRCLE' IN A THIRD COLOUR.*

MIGRATION MAZE *EACH YEAR THESE STORKS MIGRATE FROM THE NORTH TO THE WARMER CLIMATE OF THE SOUTH. CAN YOU GET FROM NORTH TO SOUTH WITHOUT TOUCHING A STORK?*

ANSWERS ON PAGE 63

For those in peril . . . A DAY WITH THE ROYAL AIR FORCE SEARCH AND RESCUE SERVICE

written by David Harwood

photographs by David Bassett
Station Photographer, RAF Brawdy

I expect many of you have seen pictures on television, or have read reports in newspapers, of RAF helicopters going on difficult and dangerous missions. They go to rescue people at sea, along the coast or at a hazardous or inaccessible place on land. The crews often risk their own lives in the service of others. There are many stories of their courage, skill and determination. But how does the Royal Air Force Search and Rescue (SAR) Service operate? What machines do they fly? What equipment do they carry? THE CUB SCOUT ANNUAL decided to find out.

We wrote to Flight Lieutenant Norman Rough, the Officer-in-charge of 'B' Flight, 202 Squadron at RAF Brawdy in Dyfed, South Wales, and asked if a few Cub Scouts could spend the day at the Search and Rescue detachment there. His reply was immediate and enthusiastic: "Of course!" Next we needed three Cub Scouts to represent you, the readers of the Annual. As the 1st Roch is an Air Scout Group attached to RAF Brawdy, we asked Mrs. Margaret Pritchard, the Cub Scout Leader, to select three boys from her Pack. And that's how David Bishopp (Sixer of the Yellow Six), Steven James (Sixer of the Green Six) and Michael Smith (also of the Green Six) went to RAF Brawdy one fine June day.

We were welcomed by Fl. Lt. Rough who introduced us to Warrant Officer Ted Little. W/O Little is a winch and radar operator in one of the SAR crews and he was to be our guide for the day. In less than no time the boys were asking questions and finding out all sorts of information about the work of the Search and Rescue Service . . .

The present Royal Air Force Search and Rescue (SAR) Wing was formed at RAF Finningley, South Yorkshire, on 1 September 1976. The Wing consists of two operational helicopter squadrons, an SAR Training Unit, a Sea King Training Unit and an Engineering squadron.

The operational squadrons carry out their SAR tasks from nine detachments around the United Kingdom mainland, providing cover for the whole of the British coastline and large areas of the surrounding seas. There is also a detachment in the Falkland Islands. The green circles indicate the areas covered by the detachments of No. 22 Squadron operating Wessex SAR helicopters, and the red circles indicate the areas covered by the detachments of No. 202 Squadron operating SAR Sea Kings.

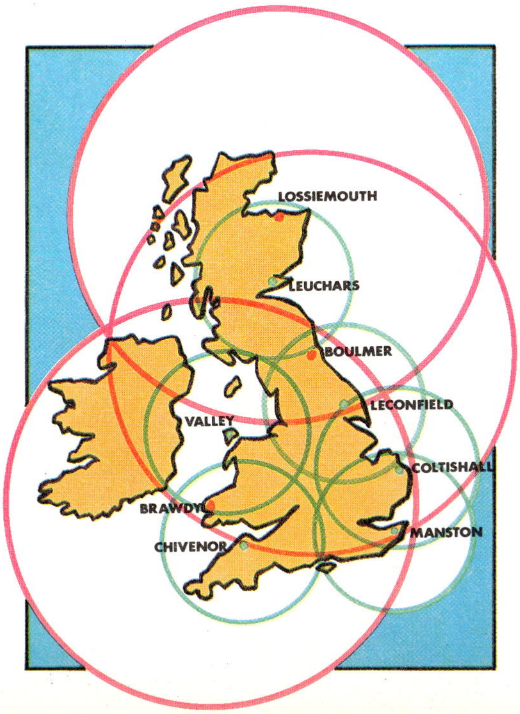

This is No. 202 Squadron's Badge. The motto *semper vigilate* means 'always watchful'. The bird is a mallard. No. 202 Squadron's association with the mallard goes back many years to the time when it had flying boats, which are aircraft which can take off and land on water. The mallard is painted on all 202 Squadron's helicopters.

The boys followed W/O Little out of the crew room into the sunshine, and walked over to a Sea King like this one. The vehicle on the left is towing a Houchin, which is a very powerful generator which provides the aircraft with electrical power to start the engines.

W/O Little pointing to one of the Rolls Royce Gnome H. 1400–1 engines. The Sea King has two engines, one on each side of the aircraft, which drive the rotor head carrying the five main rotor blades.

The boys giving the undercarriage a close inspection.They learnt that the wheels can be retracted into the sponson. The grey 'bag' on the side holds the emergency flotation bag which can be inflated by compressed air if the aircraft has to 'ditch' on water.

The Cubs took it in turns to strap themselves into the 5-point harness in the cockpit's seats. Steven (right) is sitting where the co-pilot would normally be. The co-pilot is also the navigator, but he can take control of the aircraft from his position. David (left) is in the pilot's seat.

What sort of helicopters do you have?
Here at Brawdy we have Sea Kings which are made by Westland.
How many are there here?
There's the one you can see out there on the tarmac, and there's another in the hangar. We do have a third, but that's on duty in the Falkland Islands at the moment.
Do you have any other helicopters?
Not here, no. Our Squadron, No. 202, operates Sea Kings. The other Squadron, No. 22, has Wessex helicopters.
What's the difference between the Wessex and the Sea King?
The Wessex is smaller and has a shorter range. But we don't want to sit in here talking about helicopters – come and have a look at the Sea King.

How much fuel will the helicopter take?
800 gallons. That gives it a range of about 600 nautical miles. Of course, as much of our work involves going long distances, it doesn't mean we can go 600 miles and then turn back! On the other hand we can go more than 300 miles as long as we can re-fuel. There are a number of places where we can land and take on fuel. In fact, when the need arises we'll go to unusual places like oil rigs in the sea. We have even re-fuelled from a ship at sea!
How many people can you carry?
There are seats for 17 passengers, but I have been on a mission where there were 27 people aboard, including the crew.
How long is the winch cable?
240 feet. It can be released at 200 feet a minute.

Moving towards the rear of the aircraft, W/O Little showed the boys some of the equipment a Sea King carries, including this Very pistol. 'If we think we've sighted someone, we'll fire a green flare and they'll reply with a red flare. We can also fire cartridges which give off orange smoke to show us the wind direction. I'll show you some more equipment later, but we'll look at the winch now as this machine will be going on a training flight soon.'

David getting the feel of the radar/sonar position. The radar operator has an illuminated map which shows the position of land masses and moving objects like aircraft and ships. In a Sea King SAR crew, the radar operator is also the winch operator.

W/O Little opened the sliding side door, and the boys clambered out. First they tried on the helmets and learnt that each crew member had his own, marked with his name, number and his blood group. 'The person's blood group is given in case there's an accident and he needs a blood transfusion,' W/O Little explained.

The boys then experienced what it was like to be suspended in the rescue harness.

As you can see from this photograph, taken at night, there is a great array of instruments in the cockpit. In addition to its sophisticated navigation and communications equipment, the Sea King has a Flight Control System (FCS) which allows it to hover automatically both in foul weather and at night. With the FCS in use, the winch operator can manoeuvre the aircraft by remote control from his position in the cabin doorway.

After their tour of the Sea King, the boys sat on the grass to watch the duty crew leave for a training exercise. As David was going on a special mission, he needed to put on ear muffs. The rotors began to turn. As they gathered speed, there was so much noise that the only way to communicate was by sign language. The air was whipped into a gale!

The ground crew did their final checks, the chocks were pulled away, and the marshaller signalled to the pilot that he was clear to take off. The winch operator and the winchman took up their positions by the rear door.

As David, W/O Little and the photographer battled against the wind, the Sea King rose higher into the air. The winchman was lowered to give David this unique handshake.

In the equipment rooms the boys saw the crew's special gear and clothing including life jackets, helmets and flying suits.

The helicopters carry stocks of first aid materials and equipment. Here Michael and David are looking at an oxygen cylinder and mask.

How much weight will it take?
The breaking point of the cable is 3,000 lbs, but the maximum weight we're allowed to put on it at any one time is 600 lbs, which is approximately how much three fairly heavy people weigh.

How much does a Sea King cost?
About £3 million! And it costs about £4,000 a flying hour to operate.

How many crews are there?
At Brawdy there are five crews.

How many people are there in a Sea King crew?
There are four members of the crew — the pilot, the co-pilot, the radar operator (who is also the winch operator), and the winchman.

Are you all on duty at the same time?
No. There are generally two crews available at any one time. We work a shift of 24 hours from 10.00 one morning to 10.00 the next.

What's the first thing you do when you come on duty?
The crew which is already on duty gives any information they have to the crew reporting for duty. The 'new' crew will also be given a met. briefing.

What's a met. briefing?
A meterorological briefing – which means being given details of what the weather is like in our area, and what the forecast is. Of course, the weather plays a very important part in our lives because it's often in bad weather that we are called out.

Can the weather ever be so bad that you can't take off?
Yes. Starting the rotor blades and taking off are the tricky parts. If the

The boys helped W/O Little take some pieces of equipment outside so that they could inspect them more closely. Steven was strapped and clipped into a Neil Robertson stretcher which is used for transporting and winching casualties who have been seriously injured or have broken limbs. David put on a lifejacket which was quickly inflated by a small cylinder of carbon dioxide gas. Michael slipped into a Bosun's Chair, which is usually worn by the winchman.

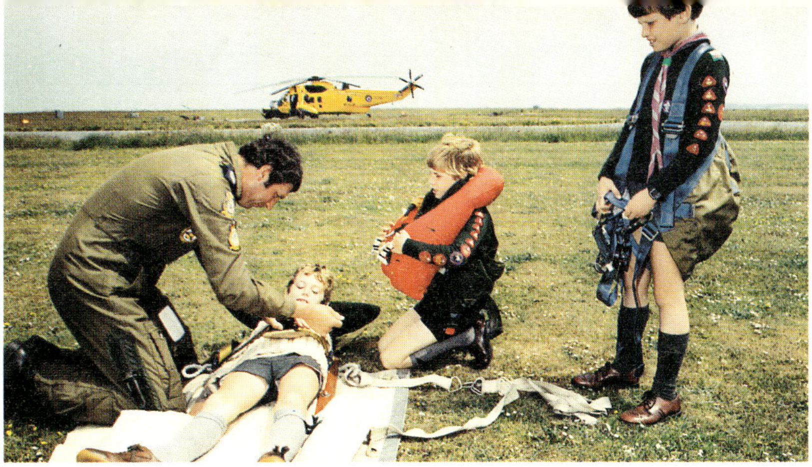

Steven is well secured in the stretcher. When the photographer asked him to wave, Steven replied: 'I can't! I've broken my arm!'

wind is blowing at more than 40 knots we can't start the rotor blades. However, once we are in the air, we can cope with almost anything!

Who tells you to go to an emergency?
All calls for assistance are relayed to one of two Rescue Co-ordination Centres (RCCs). The Northern RCC is at Pitreavie Castle, Dunfermline in Scotland, and the Southern RCC is at Mount Batten, Plymouth. The RCCs co-ordinate all Service and civilian resources in rescue operations, so a call for us to 'scramble' would come from the RCC in Plymouth.

How long does it take you to get airborne?
From the time an emergency call is received, the first standby crew has to get their helicopter into the air within 15 minutes during daylight, and within 45 minutes at night. When the first helicopter is 'scrambled', the second helicopter and its crew are brought to a similar state of readiness.

What sort of emergency are you most often called out for?
Well, the main function of the SAR Service is to assist military aircrew in distress. However, the majority of our work involves civilian rescues. We deal with incidents at sea like ships in trouble or a member of a ship's crew who is ill or injured and needs urgent medical attention. Then there are cliff falls, people in small craft in difficulties, and people on airbeds or small inflatable dinghies who have been swept out to sea by winds and currents. These inflatables can be very dangerous because they're so light that the downdraught from the rotors will throw them about, so the first thing the winchman has to do when he's lowered is to slash the airbed with a knife.

Next Steven tried on a wet suit. These suits are worn by crew members who are likely to go into the sea. They are very strong and keep out both cold and water. There are seals at the neck, wrists and ankles to make them watertight.

Steven (centre) wearing all the 'wet' gear while Michael and David are 'trying on' lifebelts recovered from two of 'B' Flight's rescue missions.

Steven needed some help to get out of the wet suit as the seals were so effective. The fine white powder on his jersey and face is from the inside of the suit. Whenever a wet suit has been in the sea it has to be thoroughly washed in fresh water. Once it is dry, the powder is sprinkled inside which enables a crew member to get into the suit very quickly.

Two views of the Operations Room. (*left*) W/O Little explaining that, on this map, the red areas mean 'danger' (for example firing ranges, power stations, etc.) and the mauve areas show where there are airfields, helicopter landing pads and places where there could be hang gliders. There are many more maps and charts stored on shelves underneath the desk. (*right*) This chart shows a Sea King's range from RAF Brawdy and the location of gas and oil rigs at which a helicopter could re-fuel.

The Communications console in the Operations Room has four radios, two telephones and a receiver for picking up aircraft distress signals. Here W/O Little is talking to the Rescue Co-ordination Centre in Plymouth . . .

. . . and then the Cubs listened in!

When the three Cubs went into the Operations Room they looked at the many maps, charts and schedules which were mounted on the walls.

An efficient communications network is also vital to the work of Search and Rescue. The SAR Operations Room at Brawdy can maintain radio contact with HM Coastguard, the Brawdy Air Traffic Control and aircraft in the air. There are also two telephones: one 'ordinary' line, and one which provides a direct link with the Rescue Co-ordination Centre in Plymouth.

The Cubs were nearing the end of their exciting and eventful day. It was time for them to leave. They all felt that they had a much better idea of what is involved in providing this emergency service which is ready, willing and able to go into action at any time.

ACKNOWLEDGEMENTS

THE CUB SCOUT ANNUAL gratefully acknowledges the help of RAF Brawdy, and in particular the personnel of 'B' Flight, 202 Squadron, without whose co-operation this feature would not have been possible.

Night and day, all year round, the RAF Search and Rescue Service is 'Semper Vigilate'.

A CUB FOR ALL SEASONS
SUMMER

Camp! The very word conjures up scenes of great adventure! Summer is the time for Cubs to go to camp to have a lot of fun as well as to learn some new skills. Of course, you have to tidy up in the morning even if it's sometimes a little chilly or raining.

Perhaps one day will have a theme and you'll do all sorts of activities based on the theme. These pirates have made their own boats, costumes and weapons . . . and it looks as though they want their tea! Camp is a great place for discovering new things — whether it's finding a grass snake in a field or exploring among the rocks on a nearby beach.

Many Scout Groups hold summer galas or fêtes to raise money for their funds. Cubs do their bit by helping to run stalls and side shows, and doing all sorts of other jobs for the good of the cause. Packs often take part in local competitions and carnivals.

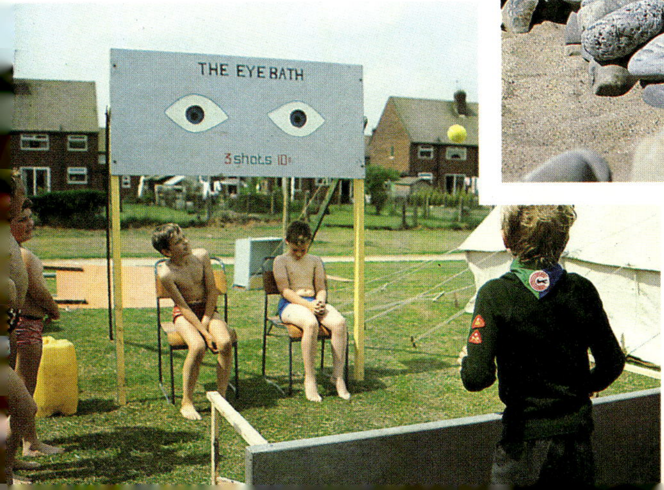

Summer means getting out and about. There'll probably be more outdoor activities during the weekly Pack Meetings, and most Packs will go on at least one outing to somewhere special, like these Cubs who are spending the day at the Severn Valley Railway. There will often be events held especially for Cubs in the District, the County and even nationally.

beginners' guide to SCREEN PRINTING

Print your own cards, posters – even tee-shirts

devised and drawn
by Malcolm Turner

With very little money, a few scrap materials, and a bit of help from an adult, you can try this basic printing process for yourself.

You will need:
Some stiff card approx. 50 cm by 30 cm (an old shoe box will do)
Pencil ★ Ruler ★ Modelling knife ★ Scissors ★ Small stapler ★
Masking tape or gummed paper tape ★ Household varnish or gloss paint ★
Household paint brush ★ Cotton organdy or polyester screen printing material (from craft shops) ★ Containers for mixing 'inks' (empty yoghurt or cream pots make ideal mixing pots) ★ soapflakes or wallpaper paste ★
Powder paints or water-based inks (from craft shops)

Carefully follow the step-by-step instructions and illustrations and you will be on your way to producing your first prints on paper or card — and even on materials and T-shirts if you buy the correct inks.

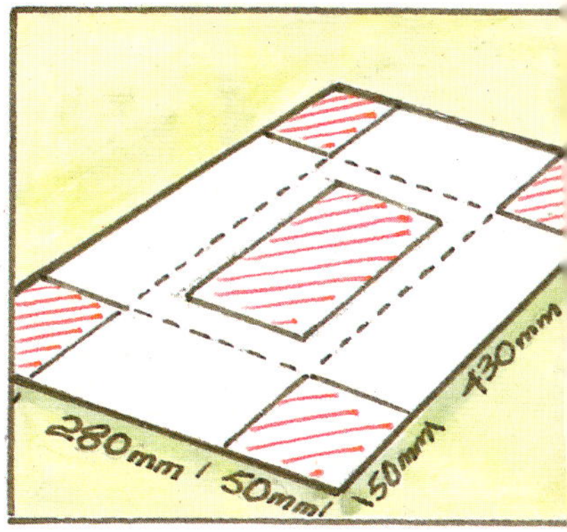

1. Mark out your piece of card as shown. Cut out the shaded areas using a ruler and a modelling knife. Score along the dotted lines with the blunt edge of the blade ready for folding.

5. Using household varnish or gloss paint, paint the box inside and out, taking great care not to get any varnish or paint on the screen mesh in the printing hole. Paint both sides of your card squeegee. Leave them to dry. The varnish or paint will make the card resistant to the water-based paints or inks you are going to use.

9. Half fill a 5 fluid oz cream pot with water. Add enough powder paint to make a smooth consistency. Then add a teaspoon of either soapflakes or wallpaper paste powder and mix in well. This should give the correct *creamy* consistency.

2. Lay the organdy/polyester screen mesh under the card and staple around the outer edges as shown, making sure you keep the material evenly stretched.

3. Fold up the four sides of the card along the scored lines and secure all four corners with either masking tape or gummed paper tape.

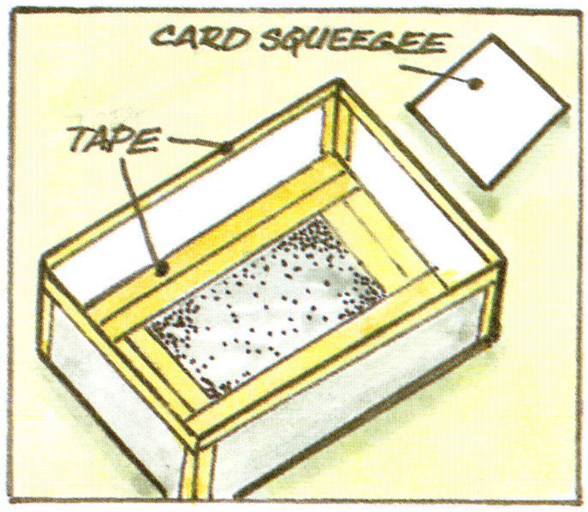

4. Tape the inside and outside of the base of the box so that a quarter of the width of the tape overlaps onto the screen mesh in the printing hole. Next, cut a square piece of stiff card the same width as the printing hole which will be your squeegee (a paint or ink spreader).

6. The next item to prepare is your paper stencil. This will be attached to the outside base of the printing box. On a piece of paper (thin paper is better) mark out the area covered by the box, and the open screen "hole". Draw your design within the screen area.

7. Place the paper on a surface which does not matter if damaged (a piece of scrap board) and cut out the design image with a modelling knife. Cut the stencil round the line marked for the base area of the box, and tape the stencil to the base of the box.

8. Tape down two pieces of card or wood on a board or old table top. These mark the position for the box and paper when it's time for printing.

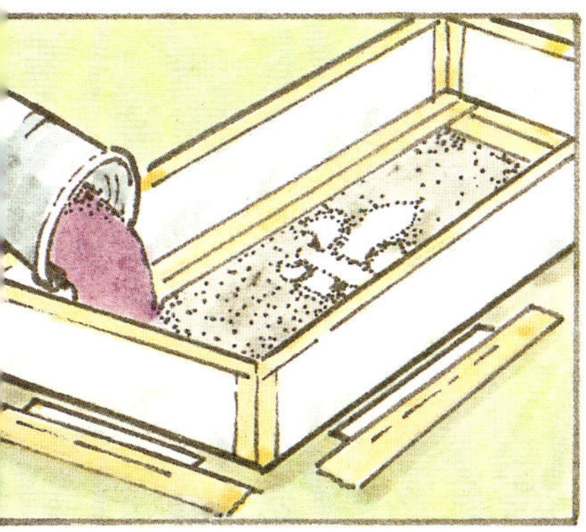

10. Take your first piece of paper and place it against the card marks on your working surface. Put the printing box in position on the top. Pour a small quantity of paint *behind* the open screen area inside the box. You are now ready to print!

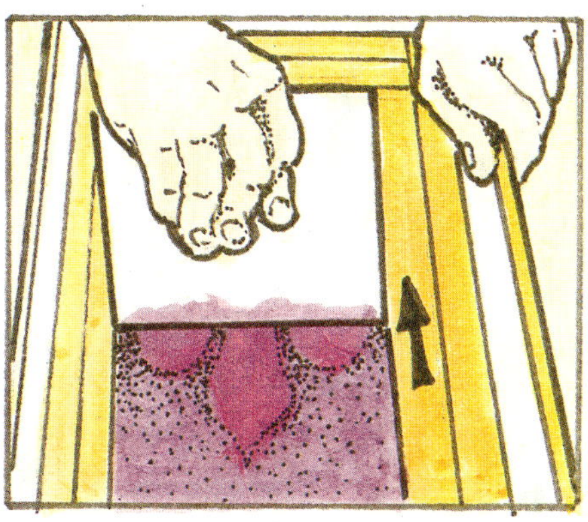

11. Place the card squeegee behind the paint and carefully pull the squeegee towards you, spreading the paint over the screen to the other end of the box. Very carefully lift the box off the paper. You should now have your first print.

12. Repeat the process as many times as you wish, adding more paint to the box when required. To clean up after printing, wash the paint from the squeegee and box with water and leave to dry. If you want to print a design in more than one colour, repeat stages **6–12** for each colour.

NABISCO

WILDLIF
CUB

TIGER The Tiger (Pathera Tigris), is one of the most impressive members of the cat family.
Habitat: Tigers are found in Central Asia, North East China, Persia, India, Burma, Malaysia, Java and Sumatra. Tigers are a greatly reduced species, with only 5-7,000 left in the wild.
Feeding: Tigers hunt whatever is available from ox or boar to deer, or fish if nothing else is available.
Breeding: Tigers usually have two or three cubs to a litter, born in secluded areas such as thick vegetation, rocks or caves. At birth the cubs are blind for three to five days. After forty days the cubs will accept meat, and after six months they will stalk their own prey.

FOX Approximately a dozen different Fox species are found throughout the world, although the Fox known to people in Great Britain is the Red Fox.
Habitat: Foxes generally live in burrows, and will hunt at night. They are very cautious animals, although some foxes are seen in towns and gardens.
Feeding: Foxes prey on small mammals, birds and fish. They also eat grass and wild fruits.
Breeding: Cubs are born in early Spring, following a 56 day gestation period. The litter is between three to eight, and the cubs are born blind. Their eyes open after a week and they are weaned by the age of two months. Cubs remain with their mothers until October and mature the following year.

BADGER The Common Badger (Meles Meles) is found throughout Great Britain and most of Europe and Western Asia.
Habitat: Badgers usually live in woodland burrows called sets near open ground, which are kept free from refuse of any kind. They create special latrines separated from the burrows. Badgers are essentially nocturnal animals, but can occasionally be seen in the morning on their way back to the burrow.
Feeding: Badgers eat earthworms, young animals and birds, and are fond of honey.
Breeding: Cubs are born in Spring and their eyes open after the first week. They are weaned at the age of one month.

these pages you can see — read about — six animals ch have young called 'cubs'. v much more can you find about these animals? How ny other animals have ng 'cubs'? What are the ng of the other animals led?
ich animals have ppies, kittens, ls, calves, etc?

This illustration was originally published as the Nabisco Shredded Wheat Wildlife Cubs Chart. It was prepared by Nabisco Ltd. with The Scout Association and devised by Aidap Marketing Ltd. THE CUB SCOUT ANNUAL gratefully acknowledges the co-operation of Nabisco and Aidap Marketing in granting their permission to reproduce the text and illustrations here.

OTTER The common Otter is found throughout Europe, North Africa, North Asia and parts of India.
Habitat: The Otter's home is burrowed out of the bank of lakes or rivers. The chamber is above water level, with the entrance below. The only openings above the water level are small air holes. These can be difficult to find and only traced by the sound of mewing cubs or the smell of fish.
Feeding: Otters eat fish, frogs, small mammals, ducks, moorhens and other birds. Otters can stay underwater for approximately four minutes.
Breeding: Two to five cubs are born in May following a nine week gestation period. They are cared for attentively by the mother.

WOLF The Wolf (Canis Lupus) is the most well-known member of the wild dog family.
Habitat: The Wolf can be found throughout the Northern Hemisphere in Europe, Asia and North America, excluding Great Britain, where they are extinct.
Feeding: Wolves run and hunt in 'packs', their prey usually large mammals. They attack young, old or weak prey, leaving the healthy to survive.
Breeding: Wolves have one litter a year. Mating takes place in January and February. Wolves' gestation lasts for two months and litters are born in thickets near pools and streams. Cubs are blind at birth and are suckled for six weeks. Cubs are fully grown at two years.

PANDA The Panda was first discovered in Western China towards the end of the 19th Century by Père David, a French missionary.
Habitat: Pandas live in Western China, where little is known about them in the wild state, although the population in the wild is estimated at approximately 600.
Feeding: Pandas live almost exclusively on vegetable food, such as bamboo shoots, but they also eat eggs and small animals.
Breeding: Many people believe the Panda to be part of the bear family, but no firm conclusion has been reached. Usually one or two young are born every year in Spring. However, very little is known about their young.

Wolf Cubbing in CANADA

by Gerry Giuliani,
National Programme Director,
Wolf Cubs,
Boy Scouts of Canada

Cubbing began in Canada in 1914, with a number of experimental Packs. By 1916, it had become an official programme and was spreading quickly across the country. As in other countries which had Scouts, considerable pressure came from communities for Scouting to offer a programme directed to boys younger than those in the Scout programme. The Wolf Cub programme was developed and based upon *The Wolf Cub Handbook* written by B.-P. in 1914, which used Rudyard Kipling's story *The Jungle Book* for its characters, its values and programme atmosphere.

A Canadian Wolf Cub sitting in front of a backdrop of characters from *The Jungle Book.*

Care and conservation — a Canadian Cub taking part in a tree planting project.

Today, there are about 100,000 Wolf Cubs in Canada. *The Jungle Book* still forms the basis for the characters and atmosphere used in the programme. There are eight programme elements of equal importance which are used to direct programme planning. These are play acting, music, star and badge work, games, crafts, outdoors and stories.

The Wolf Cub programme is developed to meet the programme objectives for Boy Scouts of Canada at a level appropriate to the age range capability of Cubs. To do this, in the Wolf Cub programme, emphasis is placed upon activities which encourage Cubs to:

- express and respond to God's love in their daily lives;
- to do their best;
- to keep fit;
- to satisfy their curiosity and need for adventure and new experiences;
- be creative and develop a sense of accomplishment;
- make choices;
- develop a sense of fair play, trust and caring

Five major theme or achievement programmes are presented through **star work**.

Each star has a set of requirements which encourages Cubs to learn about its theme by applying effort over a period of time and by selecting and working towards a series of learning goals. These five themes are:

Canadian Cubs having fun — this picture also shows the Canadian Wolf Cub uniform.
Photograph by Paul Alan Ritchi

A day out exploring at the Citidel in Halifax, Nova Scotia.

— to find out about the natural world (black star);
— to explore and take part in the organized world (blue star);
— to develop self reliance through Scouting and Scoutcraft (green star);
— care and development of yourself (red star);
— to use imagination and creative skills (tawny star)

Requirements for each of these star programmes are selected between the Cub and one of his Pack Scouters.

To help challenge Cubs in a specific and personal area of interest, twenty-six separate and varied proficiency and service badges are made available in the Cub programme. They include such badges as artist, collector, guide, handyman, pet keeper, swimmer, team player, woodsman, interpreter, and world conservation.

A Cub year would typically mean one Pack Meeting a week on a weekday evening, September to July, with about one outing every month and perhaps two weekend camps. Many Packs hold a week-long camping experience during the summer.

The Cub Pack in Canada is organized in much the same way as in the United Kingdom. It is led by Akela, the Scouter who is responsible for the operation of programming. He or she is supported by other Pack Scouters who typically assume the names of some of the other *Jungle Book* characters such as Baloo, Bagheera or Kaa. The Pack is divided into a number of Sixes to form small groups so that Scouters can better organize and administer the programme, and to help and encourage boys to learn in a smaller and more intimate type of group setting. Through the position of the Sixer, one Cub is selected to speak for the Six, and is introduced to the idea of leadership role responsibility and accountability.

Cubs all round the world are fascinated by water . . . and Canadian Cubs are no exception.

Summer fades away, and the shorter days of autumn are a signal that winter is round the corner. There's a nip in the air; the leaves on the trees turn to golds and browns before they fall; bright berries form . . .

The holidays are over and it's back to school. Most Packs will have a few weeks' break from weekly Meetings, but in September it's all 'go' again. As well as Pack night, there'll be many other activities, too . . . not least of which will be Cub League and Cup soccer matches on Saturday mornings. There's often keen competition to get into the team!

The autumn is also a popular time for the District Cub Scout Swimming Gala. Maybe you will be chosen to swim for *your* Pack. Being able to swim is very important not only so you can have fun in the water, but also because it's very healthy exercise. With some training, you can learn life-saving skills and so become prepared to cope with an emergency.

The last night of October is Hallowe' when lots of Packs hold a party. Eve one dresses up – around the coun you'll find dens of witches or wizarc vampires or some other ghostly cre tures! This is the night that ghosts a said to rise from the dead. It's an c tradition to make lanterns from turnip and to play party games – just as the Cubs are doing.

ANOTHER CUB SCOUT PUZZLE PAGE

SYDNEY SIXER AND CYRIL THE SECOND

DECIDED TO HAVE SOMETHING BEGINNING WITH 'B' – A BARBECUE! HOW MANY MORE THINGS BEGINNING WITH THE LETTER 'B' CAN YOU FIND IN THE PICTURE? THERE ARE AT LEAST 33.

CUTHBERT THE CUB SCOUT– GENUINE OR FAKE?

ON THE LEFT YOU CAN SEE CUTHBERT THE CUB SCOUT IN ALL HIS GLORY. ON THE RIGHT, THE PICTURE HAS BEEN SLICED INTO NINE PARTS, BUT SOME OF THEM HAVE BEEN 'FAKED' BY OUR ARTIST – WHICH SLICES ARE GENUINE AND WHICH ARE FAKES?

WILLIE WOGGLE WENT FOR A WALK... *AKELA WILL NEVER BELIEVE WILLIE WOGGLE WHEN HE TELLS HIM WHAT HE SAW IN THE WOODS. TO FIND OUT WHAT GAVE WILLIE SUCH A SHOCK, JOIN THE DOTS IN NUMERICAL ORDER.*

ANSWERS ON PAGE 63

by
Dorothy Kinloch,
Headquarters
Commissioner for Cub Scouts

CUB SCOUTS CARE

illustrations by Mark Viney

How many Arrows or Proficiency Badges do *you* have? If you've reached Gold Arrow stage and have an armful of badges you must be a really super Cub. Even if you are not quite so far advanced you are probably trying very hard.

All those badges, and all the activities you take part in with the Pack, help to make you a much more interesting and useful person. Have you heard the slogan "Cub Scouts Care"? It is quite difficult to live up to — but it's very good to try. The slogan was really first used to encourage Cub Scouts to help older people. It doesn't always seem a very exciting thing to do — but it can be.

When I was much younger than you, one of my favourite stories was called *The Twins Keep Shop*. I just loved that story and either read it, or had it read to me, so often that I knew it off by heart and could repeat it word for word. The twins — a boy and a girl — befriended an old man, and when he became ill, they worked in his shop and kept the business going until he got better. Of course, they had some help, but nevertheless they did a great job. It was tremendous fun for them and they learned a great deal in the process.

Another memory I have is of going with my father to visit *his* Cub Scout Leader. Miss Litton was a very tiny old lady who lived in a small dark flat. I always looked forward to visiting her. I remember that on one occasion we took a bunch of violets, bought by my Dad. You should have seen her whole face light up when she realised that they were for her. Can you imagine some day taking a present to *your* Akela?

Of course, you don't have to wait until Akela is old before you do good turns like these. There are lots of elderly people you can help *now*.

Have a chat

Many old folk live alone — or are not able to get out of the house — and there are lots of things you could do to brighten up their lives. How about calling in on your way home from school just to say, "Hello!" (But do make sure that someone at home knows what you intend doing!) Five or ten minutes is all the time you need to spend. Tell them about the sausage sizzle, the school sports, the Christmas party, your pets, and so on. You might carry in some coal, deliver the newspaper or post some letters for them. You could wash the dishes, make a pot of tea — or you might just listen while your friend talks.

Most older people enjoy a chat and you would probably learn a tremendous amount if you take the time to listen to what they have to say. They might tell you about their own childhood, the jobs they did, the sort of holidays they had and the food they ate. They might be expert in some of the things in which you are interested — stamp collecting, model railways, local history, chess, or even football — and while they probably don't know much about computers, they'd enjoy hearing all about them from you.

My neighbours are all quite elderly but I enjoy dropping in to see them. One old gentleman always gives me holly at Christmastime, and he likes me to talk about the local school. Another couple likes me to visit because *they* can tell *me* all about Canada. I've been to that vast country only once, but they have a son who lives there and have visited him often.

Last Christmas I took some mince pies to one lady and discovered that she is a much better baker than I am! Another old friend once gave me a cutting of a plant. When *she* came to visit *me* she noticed that the plant wasn't doing too well, and took it back to look after it until it was healthy. It was only then that she trusted me to look after it properly.

You see, you mustn't think that old people are useless — just as they shouldn't feel that you are too young to be of help or interest. It's up to you to show that you *can* help, and that you *do* care.

Good Luck!

The Seashore

Words by Alan Wrangles

Wherever you live in Britain, you cannot be more than about 60 miles from the nearest seashore, and what an exciting and interesting place this can be!

Every stretch of coastline has its own special character, but each will have an inter-tidal zone, which is the strip of land which lies between the high water line and the low water line.

Generally speaking the tides around the British Isles are between 3 metres and 4 metres, but there are exceptions like those in the Bristol Channel where a rise and fall of 10 metres is fairly commonplace.

Where steep cliffs plunge straight down into the sea, the inter-tidal zone is a quite narrow band along the cliff face. However, where the coastline is relatively flat, a wide strip is uncovered at low tide.

SAFETY NOTE

When you explore the seashore it is very important to remember that in different places, and at different times, the speed at which the tide comes in can change.

As "spring" tides move more quickly, you must always make sure that as it comes in, you are not being cut off from safety.

Always find out the times of the tides *before* you go on the beach. Always listen to – and take – the advice given by Coastguards and local fishermen and boatmen.

There are two main types of coastline. On the western half of Britain, it is predominantly rocks and cliffs, whereas on the eastern side wide sandy or shingle beaches are more common. There are, of course, exceptions. For example, the flat Lancashire coastline offers miles of sand, and there are those famous chalk cliffs around Dover in Kent. This variation in the type of coastline brings with it a great variety in both plant life and animal life.

Sheer cliffs, pounded by heavy surf, may well be barren except for a bed of very thick weed just under the line of the lowest tides. There may also be a very few very specialised animals like acorn barnacles which cling to the rock face.

Move around the headland and into a sheltered bay and you'll discover an explosion of life, especially if the beach has a gentle slope. Here it may be possible to see various kinds of seaweed growing in successive bands, although these different types of weed do not necessarily grow in an orderly fashion like flowers in a formal garden, but for all that it is noticeable that a change does occur.

The seaweeds growing near the high water mark of ordinary tides are those which have the greatest resistance to long exposure to sun, wind and air. Some of the plants along the low water line will be these varieties which are most vulnerable to the elements. A large number of animals use these weed beds as a refuge from predators and a shelter from the force of the waves.

Lodging on the underside of a rock overhang down towards the low water line other creatures like sea anemones, sponges and sea squirts might be found, and you may come across starfish and sea urchins in a cave. Even on the hottest day, a niche such as this provides a damp, sheltered place which is essential to this kind of animal.

However, one of the most interesting of all the many different locations on the shore is a rock pool on a coast sheltered from the prevailing wind. If all the circumstances are favourable, it is possible to discover an animal and plant population which is as varied as anywhere in the inter-tidal zone. The illustration on the next page gives you a glimpse of the wide variety of life in a rock pool.

The seashore, despite its sometimes barren appearance, can hold an extremely wide range of plants and animals, many of which cling quite precariously to life in a very turbulent region. On pages 38 and 39 you can see some of the things to look out for along a beach.

Finally, I want to give you a word of warning. We often hear of strange objects being washed up and then found on beaches. Some are harmless, others are not. If you come across metal drums, cans or sealed bottles, DO NOT TOUCH THEM. They may carry markings like those shown on page 39 but remember . . . the original markings may have been destroyed or damaged, or be covered by sand or oil. It's always better to be safe than sorry . . . so . . . LEAVE THEM ALONE!

WHAT TO TAKE

Try not to take live marine animals away from their natural home, as they will soon die. You can examine them very closely for a few minutes through a magnifying glass if you first put them into a glass jar full of sea water.

Always release marine animals quickly.

Looking at stones and shells through a magnifying glass is most interesting, and with the help of a reference book, you will be able to identify many items found on the beach.

Always carry a plastic bag to store special treasures found along the tide line as some, particularly fossils, can form the basis of a great collection.

Don't forget a notebook and pencil. . . .

The Rock Pool

If you approach a rock pool with all the stealth of a hunter you'll not only see many different kinds of seaweed, but also a host of small creatures like crabs and anemones. You must remember that virtually every animal in the pool is food either to another species, or to larger members of its own kind. Any sudden movement – even the shadow cast by a cloud (or you!) – can send these creatures scuttling to cover. They do not have brains to tell them what the different circumstances are, and their instinct is to seek shelter at once.

Illustrations by Brian Robertshaw

Key

1. Sea Gooseberry
2. Common Jellyfish. **Some of these have stinging cells which can cause a nasty itching!**
3. Stalked Jellyfish.
4. Cornish Sucker
5. Butterfly Blenny
6. Butterfish
7. Leopard Spot Goby
8. Rock Goby
9. 'Parasitic' Anemone. Not really a parasite.
10. Hermit Crab
11. Hornwrack
12. Dulse
13. Common Whelk
14. Keyhole Limpet
15. Aesop Prawn
16. Goose Barnacle
17. Thongweed
18. Common Piddock
19. Chiton
20. Shore Crab
21. Acorn Barnacle (stellatus)

When you next explore a rock pool see how many of the plants and animals illustrated here you can find.

A good way to observe these creatures in their natural habitat is to use a bucket or box which has had the bottom replaced with clear rigid plastic (see the illustration on page 35). Please remember to replace pebbles or rocks carefully. You would not like someone to take the roof off your house and not put it back, would you?

22. Acorn Barnacle (balanoides)
23. Swimming Crab
24. Sea Vase
25. Slipper Limpet
26. Serrated Wrack
27. Mussel
28. Gem Anemone
29. White Piddock
30. Brittle Star
31. Sea Slater
32. Opposum Shrimp
33. Star Ascidian
34. Common Limpet
35. Blue-rayed Limpet
36. Bladder Wrack
37. Flat Periwinkle
38. Dead Man's Fingers
39. Sea Urchin cast (dead)
40. Common Topshell
41. Carragheen
42. Common Prawn
43. Common Starfish
44. Sea Slug
45. Common Lobster

Along a Beach

A shingle or sand beach will not always offer as much of interest as a rock pool because the action of the sea creates continuous movement, so that plants cannot settle, nor can the vast majority of animals. Where there is some stability (for example, in an estuary), the tide line might well be a zone where sea asters provide an all-over pink covering to a salt marsh, and glasswort grows among the brackish dunes. Cord grass and seablite can also live in this type of habitat.

Going further down the inter-tidal zone there will be sandhoppers; peacock, sandmason and lug worms; and a host of other creatures like cockles, razor fish, green-back crabs and perhaps shrimps.

Finding these animals and plants is easier if you know where to look. For example, twirls of sand thrown up in small heaps indicate that lug worms are living in a burrow under the surface. A jet of water up to a metre high close to the low tides will betray the presence of a razor shell. Lift a boulder and you might well find a whole menagerie of animals, ranging from crabs to ragworms.

Illustrations by Brian Robertshaw

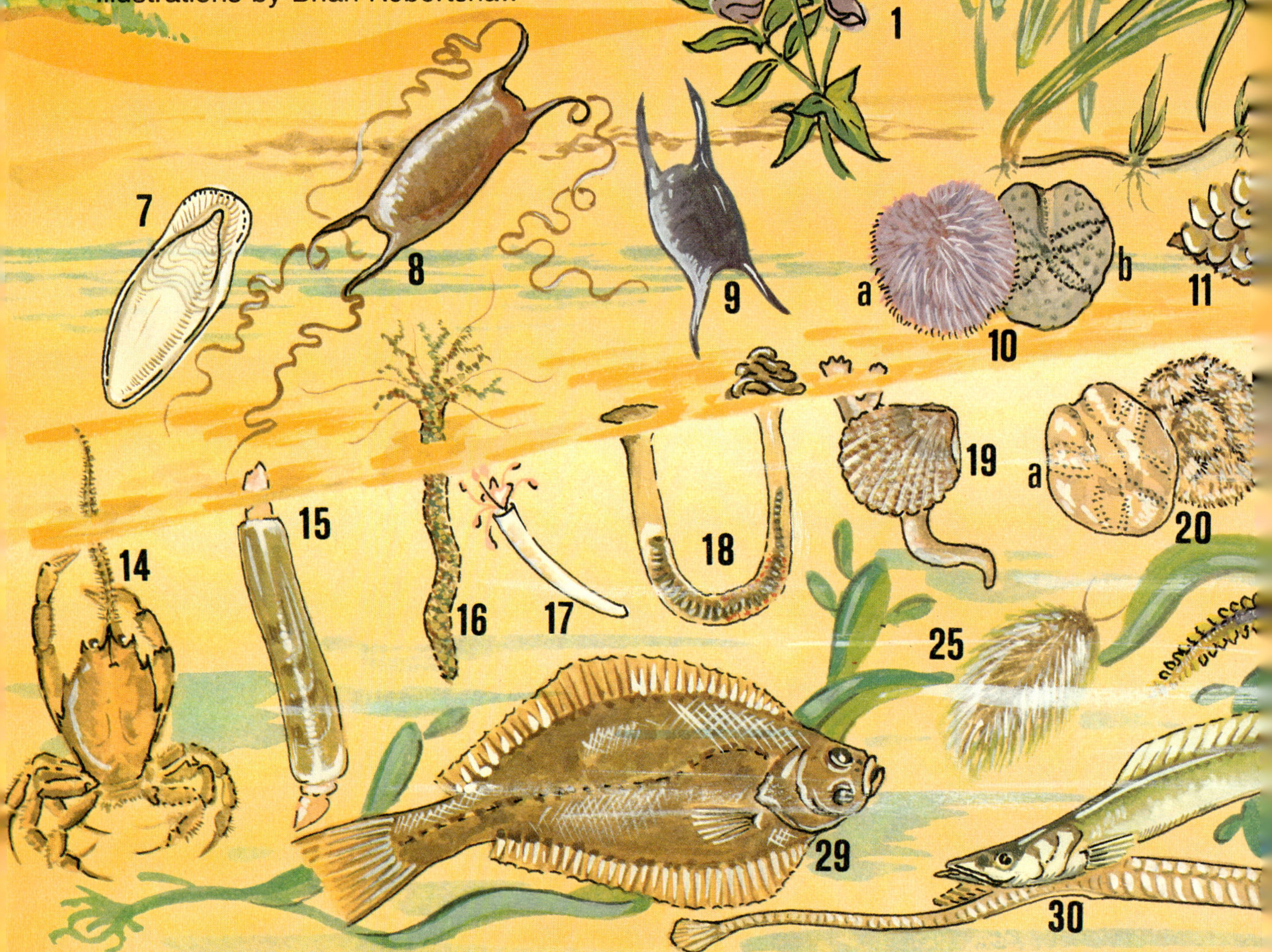

Note: Some of these creatures will also be found on mixed mud and sand or mud banks.

Key

1. Sea Pea
2. Marram grass
3. Sea Sandwort
4. Sea Holly
5. Sea Kale
6. Sea Pearlwort
7. Cuttlefish skeleton
8. Egg case of Dogfish
9. Egg case of Skate
10. Purple Sea Urchin
    a. living b. cast (dead)
11. Eggs of Dog Whelk
12. Oar Weed or Tangle
13. Labels indicating TOXIC substances.
    DO NOT TOUCH full or even apparently empty containers with these labels.
14. Masked Crab

Careful examination can reveal a mass of interesting information, but remember to look where you are going, to walk carefully, and never to destroy that which nature has taken many years to create.

15. Razor shell
16. Sand Mason
17. Tusk shell
18. Lugworm
19. Common Cockle
20. Sea Potato
    a. cast (dead) b. living.
21. Sand Gaper
22. Lancelet
23. Peacock Worm
24. Portuguese Man o' War.
    Stinging cells remain active for a long period even when stranded on beach.
25. Sea Mouse
26. Paddle Worm
27. White Ragworm
28. Ragworm
29. Flounder
30. Pipe fish
31. Sandeel
32. Lesser Weaver
    Poisonous spines on gill covers and first dorsal fin.
33. Dragonet

Coins can be stored in trays in a cabinet which looks like a miniature chest of drawers.

Collections of coins from different countries with the themes of birds (above) and animals and sea creatures (below).

How to start a ....

To start a coin collection, you must first decide which category of coins you are going to collect and how you are going to collect them.

The easiest coins to collect will be the modern ones and you will probably find that simply by checking the change in your pocket, you can build up a collection quite quickly. If you go on holidays abroad or if you know someone who travels overseas on business, you might add to your collection by sorting through the coins brought back after each visit.

You will need to set some limit on what you collect or you will run out of space and never have any money to spend on other things! This is why it is a good idea to choose a category of coins which interests you and just collect all the coins you can in that category. For example, you could collect British bronze coins (i.e. 1 penny, and 2 pence coins) or British cupro-nickel (silver) coins (i.e. 5 pence, 10 pence, 20 pence and 50 pence), with one example of each coin for each year they are minted.

If you have foreign coins, you could collect all the coins from one country or one coin from each country, or build up a collection of coins from all over the world showing birds, or animals, or trees or any other subject that you like. Another idea would be to collect coins of different shapes such as square coins, multi-sided coins or even coins with a hole in the middle.

The coins which we use every day are known as circulating coins. These have been handled a great deal after leaving the Mint and may have become scratched or damaged in use. Many collectors want the coins in their collection to be in better condition than this and they may collect the special issues of coins which are produced in qualities known as 'bright uncirculated' and 'proof'.

Bright uncirculated coins are produced in the same way as circulating coins but are specially selected and handled with care. They are packed in an illustrated folder which displays and helps to protect the coins.

Proof coins are examples of the highest quality of coin making. The dies used for these coins are polished until they shine like mirrors and the design is usually frosted so it stands out against the shiny background. The blanks are brightly polished too and each one is struck by the dies at least twice so that the design is really 'sharp'. Although the proof quality 'year' sets are struck in the same metals as the circulating coins, they are, of course, more expensive but you may think that they are worth saving up for if you are very keen on your hobby and appreciate the craftsmanship involved in producing proof coins.

When Scouting celebrated its 75th Birthday in 1982, the World Scout Foundation sponsored a limited edition of legal tender proof and uncirculated gold and silver coins. The Royal Mint was appointed to manufacture these commemorative coins and to offer them to collectors. Here you can see three

The Royal Mint produces annual sets of British coins in bright uncirculated and proof condition, each set containing a sample of all our coins. The 'year' sets are of great interest to collectors because they often contain a coin that was not available for general circulation. For example, no 10 pence coins dated 1982 were supplied to the banks because we needed fewer 10 pence coins after the 20 pence coin was introduced. The 1982 'year' sets were the only place you could find an example of the 10 pence coin with that date. Similarly, the banks had not asked for any 1984 dated half penny coins when it was decided that no more half penny coins would be struck for circulation and the 1984 example of that coin only appeared in the 'year' sets.

Commemorative coins are sometimes produced to mark special events and proof issues of these coins may be struck in precious metals such as silver and gold. Many countries had special coins to celebrate the wedding of Prince Charles and Lady Diana, and some of you may have seen the series of gold and silver coins that were struck for a number of overseas countries to commemorate 75 years of Scouting.

A serious coin collector will protect coins from damage and will keep them in special envelopes usually made of plastic. Labels on the envelopes will remind you what the coins are and will also help the person looking at your collection. There are also special albums made for coins and as your collection grows you may like to house your coins in a wooden box with trays resembling a miniature chest of drawers. Some people prefer cards with different sized holes to fit the coins. These are kept in clear plastic sleeves so both sides of the coin can be seen. By keeping the air away from a coin, it can be protected from tarnishing. Valuable coins should only be handled by the edges as fingerprints will tarnish coins.

Never clean coins to make them shine. The value of a coin can be ruined in this way. If you have a coin which you think is old and precious, take advice from an expert about how it should be cleaned or if it should be cleaned at all.

A coin collector is called a numismatist and if you can find a local numismatic society to join, you will have the opportunity to meet other enthusiasts. Most societies have details of talks and exhibitions where you could find new ideas and advice for developing your hobby.

This feature was prepared especially for THE CUB SCOUT ANNUAL by The Royal Mint.

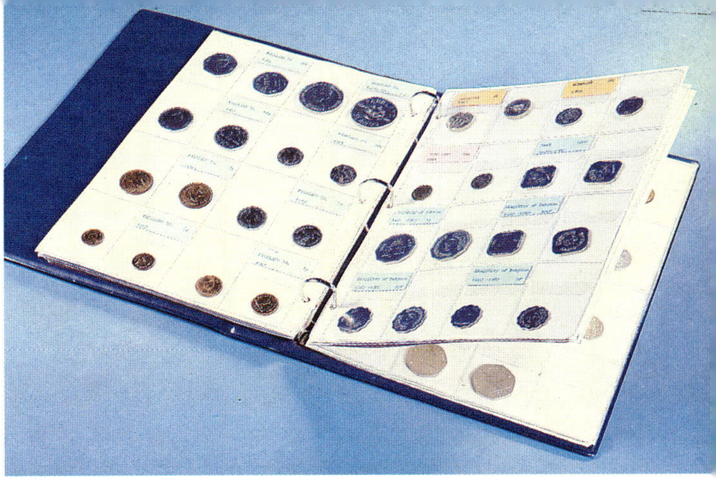

Coins can be protected in plastic see-through wallets and stored in a binder.

A collection of coins from different countries showing trees.

The 1984 United Kingdom proof coin set.

The 1984 United Kingdom brilliant uncirculated coin set.

xamples of these coins:
eft) the reverse of the silver 25p,
scension Island
ight) the reverse of the gold £2,
t. Helena
far right) the reverse of the silver 25p,
ristan da Cunha

ORRIBLE ORACE

A computer game by John Deft

What terrible news! Orrible Orace has stolen Akela's plans for the Pack camp next year! Unless they are recovered the Pack will not be able to go to camp at all. Orace has hidden the plans in his safe, and you have been chosen to try to get them back. The safe has five doors, each with a combination lock. You must not write down the combinations in case you are caught, so you will have to try to remember them.

This computer game puts you into that position. Type the program into your computer at home (or at school, if your teacher will let you) and see whether you would be able to get the plans back from Orace's safe. Most of the program will work without changes on any popular computer, but there are a few places where you may need to change the program slightly to fit your particular machine. You may want to make one or two changes, too, to make the game easier or harder. If we go through the program line by line you can see where these changes will come.

Type this program into your computer. / Program notes.

```
100 REM ################   ORRIBLE  ORACE   ################
110 REM ################   BY  JOHN  DEFT    ################
120 REM COPYRIGHT (C)1985 J A DEFT & THE SCOUT ASSOCIATION
130 REM ##################################################
```

Lines 100–130 are just the titles, and do not actually affect the running of the program at all.

```
140 CLS
```

Line 140 clears the screen. On an *Apple* computer this will need to be changed to 140 HOME and on a *Pet* or *Vic* it should be 140 PRINT CHR$(147)

```
150 PRINT "ORRIBLE ORACE HAS STOLEN AKELA'S PLANS"
160 PRINT "FOR THE PACK HOLIDAY, AND HIDDEN THEM IN"
170 PRINT "HIS SAFE. IT IS UP TO YOU TO TRY TO GET"
180 PRINT "THEM BACK, BUT THE SAFE HAS FIVE DOORS,"
190 PRINT "EACH WITH ITS OWN COMBINATION LOCK."
200 PRINT
210 PRINT "I WILL TELL YOU THE COMBINATION OF EACH"
220 PRINT "LOCK AS YOU COME TO IT, BUT AFTER A FEW"
230 PRINT "SECONDS I SHALL HAVE TO WIPE THE SCREEN"
240 PRINT "CLEAR BEFORE I AM DETECTED. THEN YOU CAN"
250 PRINT "TRY TO ENTER THE RIGHT NUMBERS, BUT BE"
260 PRINT "CAREFUL - THE SMALLEST MISTAKE WILL SET"
270 PRINT "OFF THE ALARM AND WARN ORACE!"
280 PRINT
```

Lines 150–280 give the instructions for the game, and will not need changing unless you have a very narrow screen (these lines are up to 40 characters long) or you want to change the rules in some way.

```
290 PRINT "PRESS <ENTER> TO START ...";
300 INPUT Z$
```

Lines 290–300 hold up the game to allow the player time to read the instructions. Some computers use RETURN or NEWLINE instead of ENTER in line 290 — look at your own keyboard to find out which it should be.

```
310 DIM N(6)
```

Line 310 begins the game properly by making space for up to six numbers in the

```
320 LET L=2
330 PRINT "THE FIRST DOOR IS EASY TO OPEN ...."
```

combination so that the player gets into practice for the harder ones later.

```
340 FOR I=1 TO L
350 LET N(I)=INT(RND(1)*30+1)
360 NEXT I
```

Lines 340–360 work out the actual numbers in the combination. If you have a *ZX81* or a *Spectrum*, you will need to change line 350 to read 350 LET N(I)=INT(RND*30+1) and if you are working with a *TRS-80* or a *Dragon* you will put 350 LET N(I)=RND(30) Any of these lines produces numbers between 1 and 30; you can change this (perhaps to allow numbers up to 99) by changing the 30 to some other number.

```
370 PRINT "THE COMBINATION IS:"
380 FOR I=1 TO L
390 PRINT N(I);"  ";
400 NEXT I
```

Lines 370–400 print out the complete combination on the screen.

```
410 FOR T=1 TO 300*L
420 NEXT T
```

Lines 410–420 allow time for the player to read and remember the numbers; the actual time allowed depends on the length of the combination. On a *ZX81* or *Spectrum* you will need to change 300 (in line 410) to about 90 for a sensible game, but on any machine you can increase the time allowed by increasing this number, or shorten the time by making the number smaller.

```
430 CLS
```

Line 430 clears the screen; see the notes above on **line 140**.

```
440 PRINT "NOW TRY TO OPEN THE DOOR ...."
450 FOR I=1 TO L
460 IF I=1 THEN PRINT "WHAT IS THE FIRST NUMBER";
470 IF I>1 THEN PRINT "WHAT IS THE NEXT NUMBER";
```

Lines 440–470 invite the player to enter, one by one, the numbers in the combination as he remembers them.

```
480 INPUT M$
490 LET M=VAL(M$)
```

Lines 480–490 take in the player's numbers; these two lines could be replaced by a single line 480 INPUT M but doing it this longer way will stop the program from breaking down if the player types a letter instead of a number.

```
500 IF M=N(I) THEN GOTO 550
```

Line 500 checks each number to see if it is right.

```
510 PRINT "CLANG!!!!!!!!  THE ALARM HAS GONE OFF!"
520 PRINT "I CAN HEAR ORACE IN THE CORRIDOR ...."
530 PRINT "ESCAPE QUICKLY AND COME BACK LATER!"
540 GOTO 670
```

Lines 510–540 sound the alarm if the player makes a mistake. If your computer has sound facilities, you might like to add some extra lines here to produce a suitable 'alarm' noise.

```
550 PRINT "CLICK!"
560 NEXT I
570 PRINT "THE DOOR SWINGS OPEN...."
```

Lines 550–570 react to the correct numbers typed in by the player.

```
580 FOR T=1 TO 100
590 NEXT T
```

Lines 580–590 give a short delay after the combination is complete; you will probably want to change 100 to about 30 on a *Spectrum* or *ZX81*.

```
600 LET L=L+1
610 IF L>6 THEN GOTO 640
620 PRINT "BUT THERE IS ANOTHER DOOR BEHIND IT!"
630 GOTO 340
```

Lines 600–630 make the next combination one number longer, unless all the doors are now open. You can change the difficulty of the game by changing the 6 in line 610, but this number must agree with the number in line 310.

```
640 PRINT ".... AND THERE ARE AKELA'S PLANS. WELL"
650 PRINT "DONE, SUPERCUB - THE PACK CAN GO TO"
660 PRINT "CAMP AFTER ALL!"
670 PRINT
680 END
```

Lines 640–680 mark the end of the game, when all the doors are open. You might want to add some noise or flashing lights here, but that is up to you.

Remembering messages and telephone numbers is something that every Cub Scout should be able to do, and with this game you can practise remembering and have some fun at the same time. Good luck!

The Winners!

Paul Kemshell with the train set he bought from the money he won in the competition. (photograph by The Reporter, Dewsbury)

There was a large entry in the 1984 CUB SCOUT ANNUAL's 'Name These Tunes' Competition. We gave the opening bars of music of 12 well known songs, carols and hymns, and competitors were asked to give the correct titles.

It was a competition with a difference because competitors were asked to let us know what they would choose as First Prize (up to £100), Second Prize (up to £50) and Third Prize (up to £25).

We put all the correct entries into a 'hat' and Dorothy Kinloch, the Headquarters Commissioner for Cub Scouts, made the draw at Baden-Powell House in London.

The first entry form to be drawn came from Paul Kemshell of the 4th Dewsbury Pack in West Yorkshire. For his prize he chose a Hornby railway track and two locomotives. Paul was only eight when he entered the competition. He felt that the railway would be something which the whole family could enjoy.

Second Prize went to Christopher Gray of the 2nd Chester-le-Street (St. Mary and St. Cuthbert) Tuesday Pack in County Durham. As he is a keen bird watcher, and a member of the Young Ornithologists Club, he spent his prize money of £50 on a pair of binoculars.

The Third Prize of £25 was won by David Oswald of the 14th Perthshire, Bridge of Earn Pack in Scotland. David added some birthday money to the prize and bought a radio-cassette recorder.

There were 25 Runner-Up Prizes of The International Cub Scout Book and The Outdoor Adventure Book.

The Competition was sponsored by World International Publishing Limited (the official Annual publishers of The Scout Association).

There's another great competition this year — turn to page 58 and have a go!

The Wood Quiz

How many objects which are made from wood can you find in this illustration?

Answers on page 63

A CUB FOR ALL SEASONS
WINTER

When does winter begin? Maybe it's at the end of October when Summer Time ends and we have to turn the clocks back an hour, or perhaps it's when there's a sudden cold spell, or maybe you think it begins on Bonfire Night. Talk of winter and many people mention ice and snow. However, in the southern part of the UK at any rate, the snow doesn't often last for long . . . but of one thing you can be sure . . . wherever and whenever it does appear, Cubs make sure they make the most of it!

At the beginning of November lots of Cubs will be celebrating Guy Fawkes Night. This fireworks and bonfire party was organised by a Scout Group: several Packs went along to enjoy a spectacular fireworks display and a blazing bonfire.

A Cub Scout helps other people all the year round, but at Christmastime, many Cubs – individually, in small groups or as a Pack – make an extra effort to do some Special Good Turns . . . visiting the elderly, making and delivering food hampers for pensioners, carol singing for a good cause, taking presents to children in hospital or to those who otherwise would not have many gifts to open on Christmas Day.

The winter, too, is the time for indoor activities – Gang Shows, trips to the theatre and parties. Many Packs have a Christmas Party. This Pack had one with a theme . . . each of the boys could dress up as a character who had something to do with the festive season. How many of the characters can you recognise here?

As January gives way to February, and February leads into March, the days grow longer; trees and plants and bushes which have seemed to be dead for months start to show signs of life . . . spring begins . . .

How to play the GRAB A LETTER GAME on the back cover

This is a new and exciting game which can be played by almost any number of players. You can even play it on your own! The idea of the game is to choose a word you want to spell. You then throw a dice to move a counter round the board until you have collected the letters you need to make the word. There are a number of variations of the game, too, so you can get a lot of fun from using the board.

Equipment you will need
A dice
A small object or counter for each player
Paper for writing down words and scores
Pens or pencils

About the Board
BLUE SQUARES count as any letter of a player's choice
GREEN SQUARES mean that a player can have an extra turn
RED SQUARES cannot be passed over or landed on
THE PICTURE SQUARES cannot be passed over or landed on

How to Play
1. All players place their counters on the START picture square in the centre of the board.
2. Players should decide how many letters the words for a particular round should have, but words should have at least three letters.
3. Each player chooses a word containing the number of letters decided (2).
4. Each player writes down his word clearly on a piece of paper and places it in front of him so that all players can see each other's words.
5. For this basic game a player must collect the letters in the order in which they appear in his word. (For example, if the word is SCOUT, a player would need to collect 'S' first, then 'C', then 'O', then 'U' and finally 'T'.)
6. Each player takes it in turns to throw the dice and move his counter out of the START for the number of squares shown on the dice. He may leave the START from any point he wishes, but for each 'go' a player can move his counter only in a straight line (i.e. sideways, upwards, downwards or diagonally).
7. A player's next move is from the square on which he has landed. It will often take several moves to collect a particular letter. There cannot be more than one counter on a square at the same time.
8. A player *must* move his counter the number of squares indicated on the dice. He cannot miss a turn.
9. The winner of a round is the player who is the first to collect all the letters to make his word.

VARIATIONS
There are other games you can play on the Grab a Letter Board . . .

CRISS-CROSS
Play the game as described, but the counters can be moved only sideways, upwards or downwards.

DIAGONALS
Play the game as described, but counters can be moved only diagonally: this makes the game more difficult.

FOUR CORNERS
A game for up to four players. Play the game as described, but each player starts from one of the small picture squares instead of the large centre square.

TAKE SIX
Place counters at the START. Players take it in turns to throw the dice six times, and move their counters (as described in 6 – 8 above) to collect six letters. For this game, BLUE SQUARES count as blanks (no letter). Each player then makes the longest word he can from the letters he has collected. A six letter word scores 6 points, a five letter word 5 points and so on.

COLLECT THE ALPHABET
Write down all the letters of the alphabet on a piece of paper. By moving the counters (as described in 6 – 8 above) cross off the letters as you collect them. You can *either* collect the letters in any order *or* (much more difficult and challenging) collect them in their correct sequence (i.e. A, B, C, D, etc.). For this game, BLUE SQUARES count as blanks (no letter).

SOME OTHER KNOTS

by Eric Franklin

illustrations devised by Eric Franklin and drawn by Stephen Roberts

If someone asked you how many knots you thought there were, what would be your guess? Dozens, hundreds, thousands? In actual fact there are only six which are:

No. 1. The knot for tying the ends of the same rope together.
No. 2. The knot for tying two different ropes together. This is called a *bend*.
No. 3. The knot for making a loop in a rope.
No. 4. The knot for fastening a rope to a post, ring, etc. This is called a *hitch*.
No. 5. The knot for temporarily shortening a rope.
No. 6. The knot for making a stopper or knob in the end of a rope.

Eric Franklin is the author of *The ABC of Knots*, published by Brown, Son and Ferguson.

This list does not include fancy knots and knots which are tied solely for decorative purposes. All the many knots listed and described in books on knotting are variations of the six given above and the variations are very extensive. The famous *Ashley Book of Knots* has 3,854 numbered paragraphs and each paragraph has from one to several illustrations relating to it. So let us look at just a few of these variations.

There is not much we can do with No. 1, because about the only knot for joining ends of the same rope is the REEF KNOT, which I am sure you can tie already. So let's turn to No. 2! There is no better knot for tying two ropes together than the SHEET BEND as long as the two ropes are of similar thickness. If one rope is thicker than the other, we would tie a DOUBLE SHEET BEND. If one rope was very much thicker than the other it would be advisable to 'seize' the end of the thick rope to its standing part. However, in the last instance, it would be better to use a RACKING BEND in which racking turns (which are figure-of-eight turns) are taken in and out of the loop formed in the large rope.

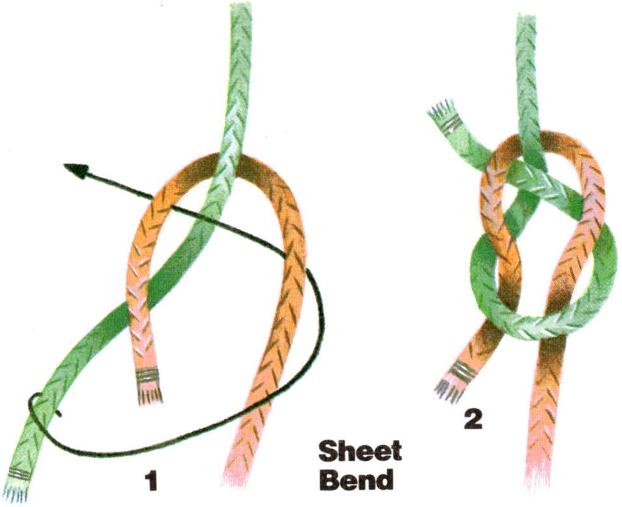

Sheet Bend

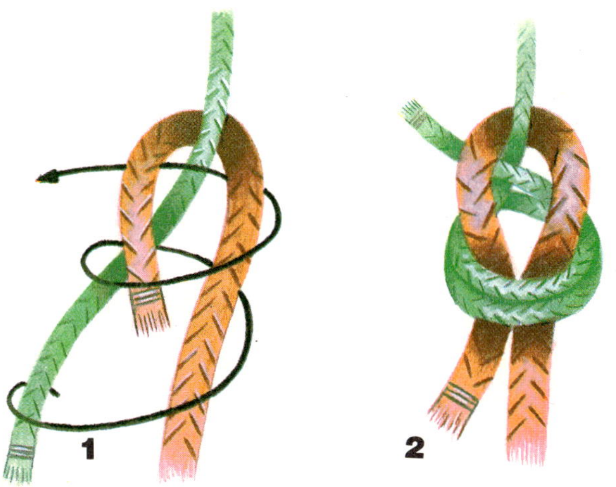

Double Sheet Bend

Double Sheet Bend Seized

Racking Bend

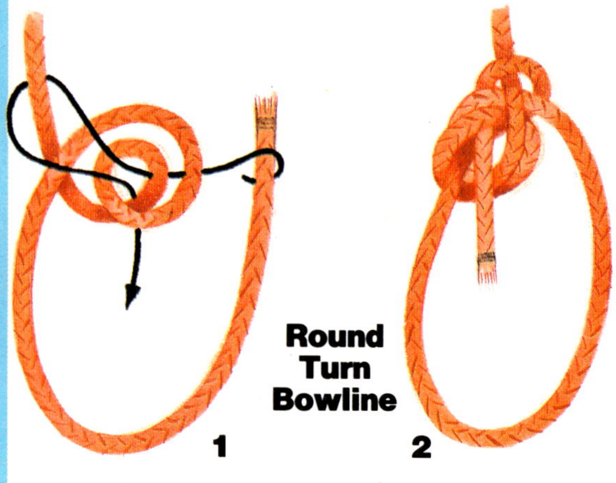

Round Turn Bowline

There is much more variation when it comes to No. 3 — making a loop in a rope. Sooner or later you will be expected to learn to tie a BOWLINE and, perhaps later, a BOWLINE-ON-A-BIGHT, but I'll bet that you didn't know that there are more than twenty different bowlines! For a single loop there is a ROUND TURN BOWLINE which is similar to a DOUBLE SHEET BEND. For multiple loop knots there are the FRENCH BOWLINE, the PORTUGUESE BOWLINE, the SPANISH BOWLINE and several more.

The ROUND TURN BOWLINE is supposed to be rather more secure than the normal bowline, particularly if the rope is wet and/or slippery. The bowlines with two loops are regularly used as rescue knots with the casualty being suspended in one way or another in the two loops; most of them have the two loops hanging parallel, but the SPANISH BOWLINE has the two loops splayed.

Another use is for temporarily suspending a man over the side of a ship for painting or repairing purposes. You could also use one in the end of a tent's guy line in order to use two tent pegs for extra security on soft ground.

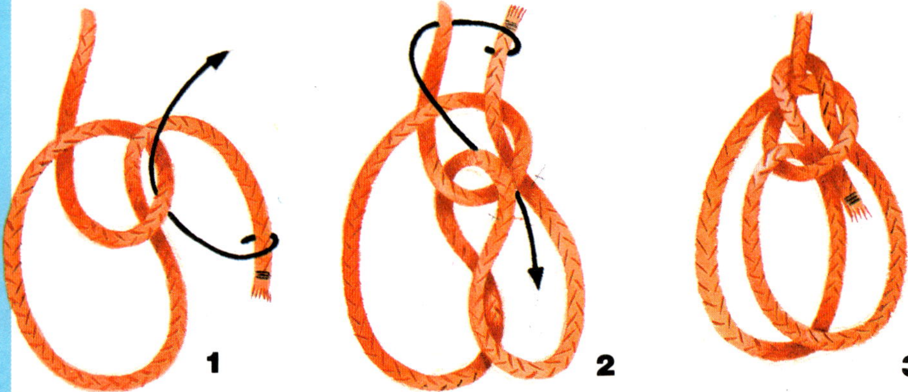

French Bowline

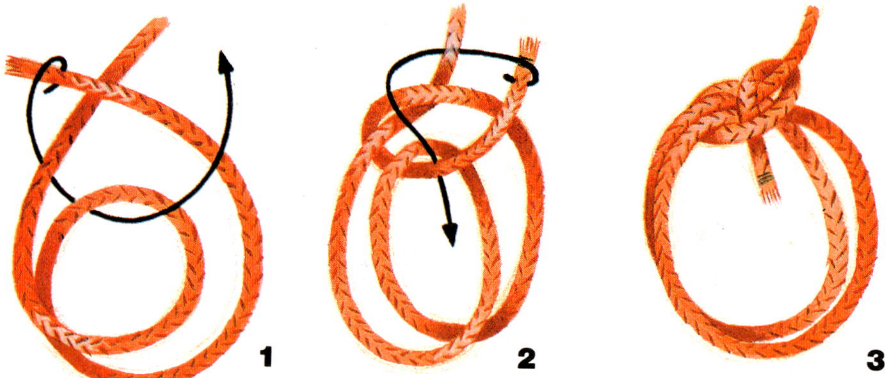

Portuguese Bowline

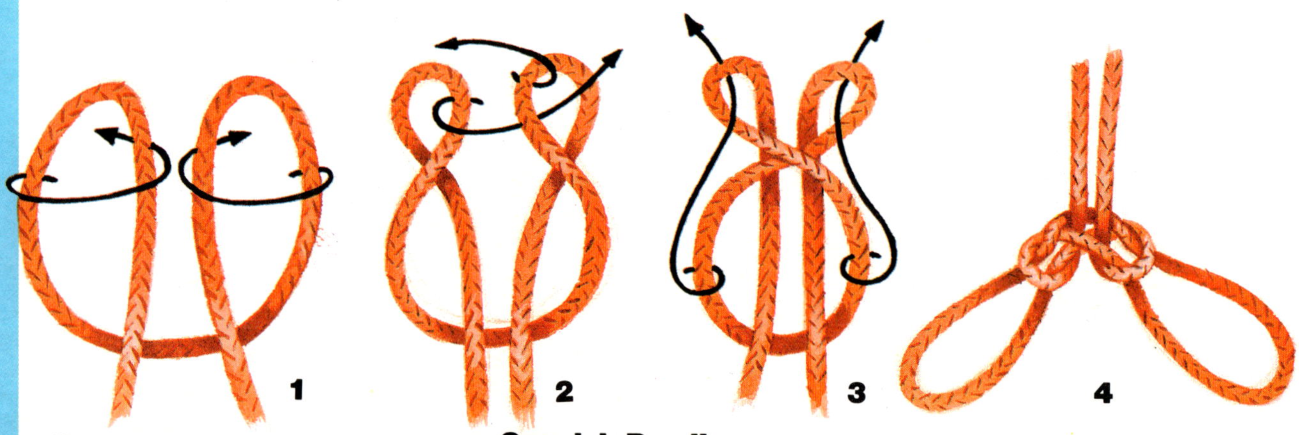

Spanish Bowline

Now for No. 4 — knots for hitching a rope to a post, spar or ring. There are very many knots for doing this. You will be expected to learn to make a ROUND TURN AND TWO HALF HITCHES and a CLOVE HITCH in due course, and these are excellent knots, but have you heard of the ROLLING HITCH or the MIDSHIPMAN'S HITCH? Actually, these two knots are identical in form, but the ROLLING HITCH is made round a larger object such as a hawser (heavy rope) or a post, while the MIDSHIPMAN'S HITCH is made round its own standing part. The value of these two knots is that the knot will not slip when the pull is at a sharp angle rather than at right angles.

The ROLLING HITCH is regularly used for hauling a large, heavy rope by means of a light line, but it can also be used on stays for, say, a flagstaff.

The MIDSHIPMAN'S HITCH is a useful rescue knot when a rope is thrown to a man overboard (he makes a loop round himself using the hitch) and in camp it also makes an excellent guy-line hitch to replace a slider. The BACKHAND HITCH is another simple knot: a loop instead of an end is passed through a ring or round a spar, and the end slipped through and then hitched to the standing part.

There seem to be fewer variations of No. 5 knots — those for temporarily shortening a rope. The SHEEPSHANK is the basic shortening knot, and I have shown two variations of it.

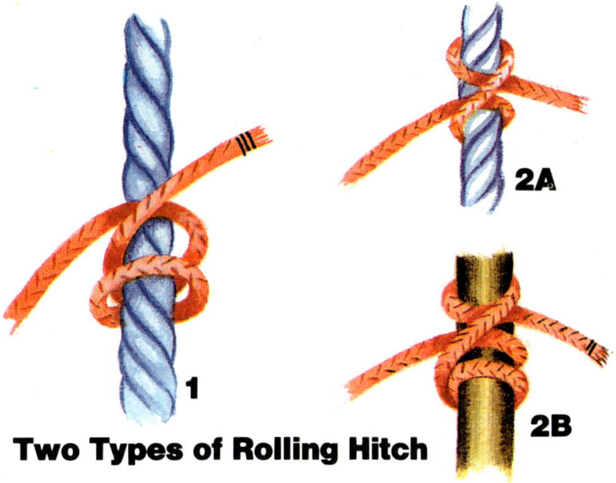

Two Types of Rolling Hitch

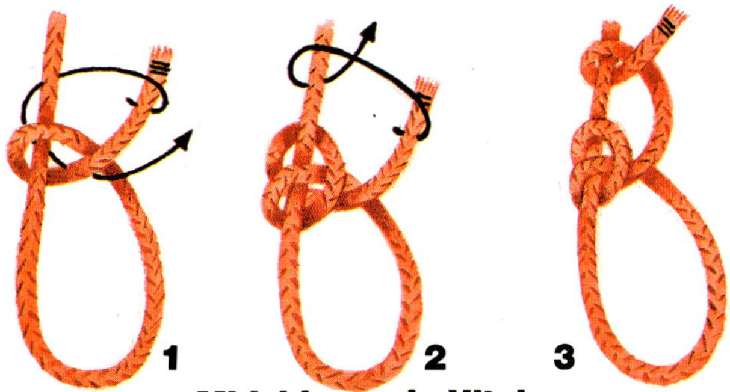

Midshipman's Hitch

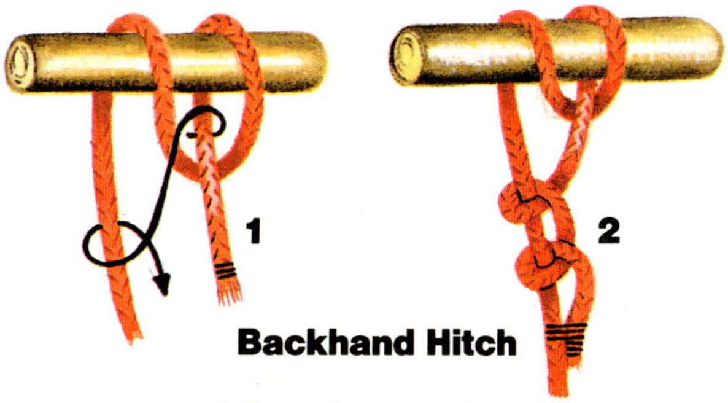

Backhand Hitch

One sort of Sheepshank

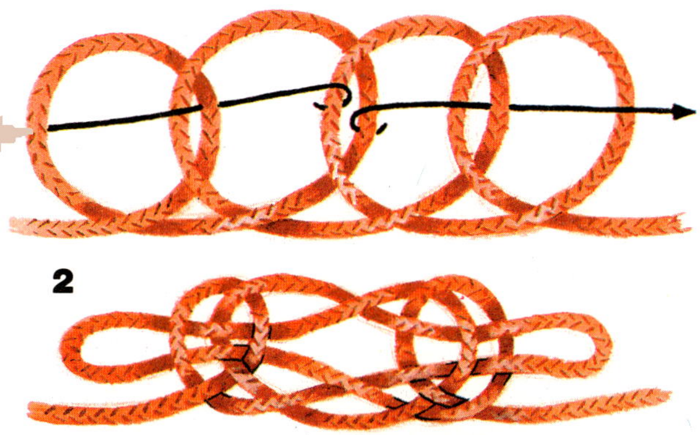

Another sort of Sheepshank

For No. 6 knots there are so many knob knots that it would seem they include all possible variations! With the exception of the THUMB KNOT and the FIGURE-OF-EIGHT KNOT, most of them are formed by unlaying the rope and making the knot with the individual strands. These knots are a bit more complicated to tie, and there isn't space to show them here this year. If you are interested, look for the WALL KNOT, the CROWN KNOT and the MAN ROPE KNOT in a knot book.

I have shown you just a few of "the other knots". Now it is up to you. You could have a lot of fun looking for more variations on our six basic knots — in knot books, on a visit to an old ship like *H.M.S. Victory* in Portsmouth, those in London's St. Katharine's Dock, or those in other maritime museums around the country. Tying knots is always a lot of fun.

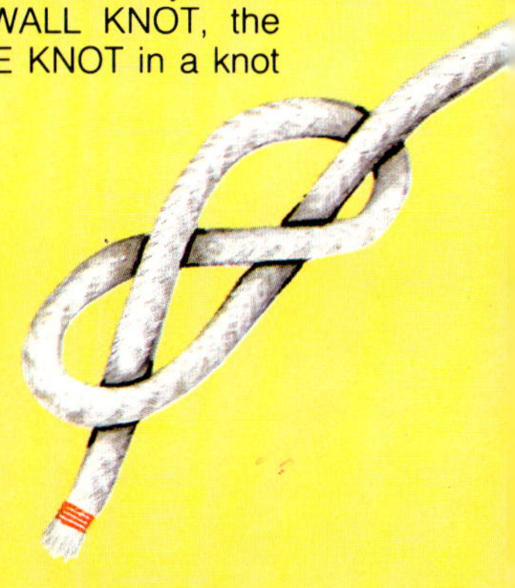
Figure-of-Eight Knot

Fact or Fiction?

Cowboys and Indians in the Movies

How often have you seen the hostile Indians suddenly appear on the surrounding heights while, down below, the wagon-train or the stage-coach pulls up in horror as they realise the danger? It makes good cinema, but did it ever happen? Well, of course not! Just think! If YOU set an ambush, would YOU suddenly appear and let everybody see you and give them time to form the wagons into a circle, or race away before you could get down off the hill and give chase? Indian attacks were usually carried out by fairly small raiding parties which would keep under cover, waiting to dash in suddenly, inflict the maximum damage and dash away before any of the whites had time to shoot back.

Written and illustrated by Frank Humphris

This is another scene popula in early films. The wagons ar corralled and the pioneers ar shooting from between th wagons as the Indians rid round and round apparentl waiting to be shot off thei horses. It might have mad sense in the muzzle-loadin era, for having caused the de fenders to empty their guns the Indians might hope to rush in while the pioneers were re loading. However, it is a matte of record that far more people died from illness — some even from starvation — or were drowned crossing rivers, than ever died from Indian attacks.

On the almost treeless prairies, many early settlers and cowboys lived in a shack which was half dug-out and half built of clods of earth, laid one on top of the other. The few pieces of wood brought along were used to support the roof. It was hard and miserable in the extreme. Cloth was home-spun and clothes home-made. There was no schooling and few of the pioneers could read or write.

Most of the pistols and rifles used in the early West were percussion or muzzle-loading guns. Metallic cartridge firing revolvers and the popular .44 Winchester both appeared in 1873.

Some film makers ignore this and one sees examples where, in scenes supposedly taking place just after the American Civil War (1861–1865), everyone is carrying guns not invented for another eight years!

But the muzzle-loader was *slow*. Here you see two of the operations necessary for loading.

USING THE RAMROD TO PUSH THE BULLET DOWN THE BARREL.

FRANK HUMPHRIS IS HERE SHOWN POURING POWDER INTO THE FLASH PAN OF A KENTUCKY RIFLE IN PREPARATION FOR FIRING. THE BARREL HAS ALREADY BEEN LOADED WITH POWDER AND BALL.

John Sweet invites you to try some

PARTNER ACTIVITIES AN

illustrated by Peter Harrison

Matching your skill and strength against someone else can be great fun. On these pages you will find some ideas to try out with a friend. Do remember to be sensible when doing these activities — the idea is *not* to hurt your partner!

ARMS LOCK WRESTLE Partners sit back-to-back with knees bent. Elbows locked so that one is over that of partner and the other is under that of partner. Partners then try to get each other's upper arm sideways on to the floor.

DUCK FIGHTING Partners in crouch position with hands up and flat palms facing (holding the other's hand and interlocking fingers are *not* allowed). Jump about, keeping knees bent to try and make partner put his hands down or sit down.

ARMS LENGTH TOUCH Opponents toe two lines about one metre apart. Each tries to touch the other without moving his feet.

DANISH WRESTLE Partners grasp right hands, with right foot forward and the outsides of feet together. Without releasing hand-hold, pull or push with arm to make partner move the forward (right) foot.

TITCH...CUB SCOUT

by Leslie Ceci

CONTESTS

CHINESE GET-UP Partners back-to-back with arms locked. Without moving feet, sit down and get up by knees bending and stretching.

ARMS LENGTH PRESS Opponents face each other. One has arms outstretched in front, while the other tries to push hands together within a count of five.

COCK FIGHT Sit facing opponent with knees bent and legs crossed. Grasp own ankles. Keeping hands on ankles and without uncrossing legs, opponents push at each other's toes, attempting to lift opponent's feet from the ground.

HANDS PULL APART Boy on left closes hands in front of himself as his opponent catches hold of his wrists to try and pull hands apart within a count of five.

INDIAN WRESTLE Partners lie side by side, heads to tails. Swing inside legs up to vertical, ankles locked. Keeping legs straight and arms on the floor, each tries to roll the other backwards.

TITCH . . . CUB SCOUT

by Leslie Cecil

A Typical Cub Scout

In the 1984 Cub Scout Annual, v
asked the question: "Is there
typical Cub Scout?" and aske
you, the readers, to show us wh
you thought a typical Cub Scou
looked like. We had lots and lots o
entries, and it was a very difficu
job to choose the "Top Ten". Bu
here they are! Each of the Cu
artists has received a free copy o
this 1986 Annual. There's anothe
Challenge this year (see page 62

MARCUS WINTERS - Mansfield Woodhouse (Elm) Pack - NOTTS

Based on an idea by MARK BAILEY Walldown Pack Bordon - HANTS

CHRISTOPHER LAMBOURNE 3rd Pembroke Pack - DYFED

GREGOR COLQUHOUN 1st Inverbervie Pack - ANGUS

HARVEY COSSELL
1st Herne Bay Pack - KENT

DAVID EYRE
1st Liphook Pack - HANTS

STEPHEN HEMSTALK
17th Tonbridge (Rowallan) Pack - KENT

OLIVER LEIGH
13th Selby Pack - N. YORKS

MARTIN STANIFORTH - 1st Wydale
52nd Scarborough Pack - N. YORKS

ANDREW McDADE
Churchdown (Blue) Pack - GLOS

The Farmer's Will

by Eric Franklin

Once upon a time a farmer called Seamus O'Leary lived in a small village in a remote part of Ireland. He had three sons. When he died, all he had to give to his children was a herd of cattle. He also left a rather peculiar Will which he had given to the parish priest.
The Will read as follows:

This is The last Will and Testament of Seamus O'Leary

When I am buried, go to my desk and take out the pack of cards I always played with. Go through the pack and take out three Aces – the Ace of Hearts, the Ace of Diamonds and the Ace of Clubs. Leave the Ace of Spades alone as that is different. Lay the three Aces in a row and then deal the next three cards so as to make three fractions. My cattle are to be divided amongst my three sons in those proportions.

Signed S. O'Leary

The sons promptly carried out these instructions only to find that the next three cards were a two, a three and a nine, thus making fractions of one half, one third and one ninth. They then went out and counted their father's cattle. There were only seventeen animals. But how could anyone divide seventeen cows into a half, a third and a ninth?

They took their problem to the parish priest, who was the cleverest man in the village. He thought for a few minutes and then said, "I will lend you my one cow so that you have eighteen and then you can divide them up." So the priest lent the brothers his one cow and then counted out one half of the animals, i.e. **nine** for the eldest brother; then one third, i.e. **six** for the middle brother; and finally one ninth, i.e. **two** for the youngest brother.

"There you are," the priest said. "That's just right. Nine plus six plus two equals seventeen. You have your dear father's seventeen animals and I can take back the one I lent you." And everyone was happy.

Now you have a go . . .

You may think it enough just to tell the story but it's much more fun if you illustrate it. Here's what to do.

1

Take out any two, three and nine cards and then a Joker from a pack. Place these four cards on the *top* of the pack in that order. Replace the cards in their case and put them in a drawer ready for use.

2

When the time comes to tell the story to your friends, go to the drawer and take the cards out of their case. As you get to the part of the Will which says ". . . take out three aces . . ." start running through the pack, faces towards you, and as you locate each ace place it on top of the pack so that eventually the three top cards are aces. Of course, you must be careful not to disarrange the four special cards you have previously put on top.

Now you turn the pack over and deal the three aces on to the table side by side.

4

As you continue the story, lay the next three cards out (the two, the three and the nine), one on top of each ace, thus forming the fractions ½, ⅓ and ⅑.

5

When you get to the part where the Priest lent the brothers his one cow, you deal eighteen cards face down in front of you. **Place the rest aside.** You will remember that you had placed a Joker fourth from the top and therefore, as you deal out eighteen cards, this Joker becomes the *bottom* card.

6

Now continue with the story using the pile of 18 cards. As you tell how the priest counted nine animals you count off nine cards and place them by the appropriate fraction. As he counted six animals, you count off six cards by the middle fraction. Finally count off the two and leave the last card face down on the table.

7

As you finish the story, casually turn over this last card, reveal it as a Joker and remark: "You know, I think that man was something more than a village priest!"

A LAST TIP

If you are at a friend's house and haven't got a prepared pack of cards, do not worry. You will remember that you had to turn the pack face up and look for the three aces. Well, there are four each of the twos, threes and nines and you can quite quickly locate one each of these while you look for the aces and slip them to the top without anyone noticing. If you come upon an ace early in the search pass it by to give you more time and come back to take a second look. With a little practice you will find you can locate all the cards you want and place them in position without raising any suspicion that you are doing anything other than finding the aces.

Name the Flags

FIRST PRIZE

Sinclair Spectrum+ computer

SECOND PRIZE

Sinclair Flat Screen TV

Scouting has spread right round the world. Today there are more than 16 *million* Scouts in over 150 separate territories. So, as a Cub Scout, you really are a member of an international Brotherhood. But how much do you know about countries other than your own? We're giving you the chance to show us a bit of your knowledge by identifying some countries' flags. If you can name the countries correctly and solve a little problem, you could be a Cub Scout who wins a great prize!

Here's what to do

1. Look at the flags which are illustrated on the opposite page. First, correctly identify the name of the country to which each flag belongs and write its name under the flag, putting the first letter in the box provided. (By the way, we know that one flag appears three times — that's because there are very few countries which begin with this letter!) When you have done this, take the first letter of the name of each country in the order in which the flags appear. These 15 letters will give you four words of a sentence: we want you to complete the sentence correctly. We've given you a start by doing the first one for you. One final clue — 3, 5, 5, 2.
2. On the Entry Form on page 61:
   a. Write the names of the countries in BLOCK CAPITALS in the numbered boxes. We've put a box for the first letter of each answer to help you to 'de-code' the words in the incomplete sentence.
   b. Put the first letter of each answer in the boxes shown and then . . .
   c. Complete the sentence!
   d. Fill in your name, address, date of birth and Cub Scout Pack.
3. Carefully cut out the Entry Form along the broken lines (or take a photocopy of the page if you do not want to cut out the page) and send it, to arrive not later than Friday, January 31, 1986, to:
   1986 Cub Scout Annual Competition
   Editorial Department
   The Scout Association
   Baden-Powell House
   Queen's Gate
   LONDON
   SW7 5JS

The Rules

1. All competitors must be under the age of 11 years on December 31, 1985.
2. The closing date for the competition is Friday, January 31, 1986.
3. All the entries will be placed in a sack. The FIRST PRIZE will be awarded to the first complete, correct entry to be drawn at a date to be arranged in February 1986. The SECOND PRIZE will be awarded to the second complete, correct entry to be drawn, and so on.
4. Prizewinners will be notified by post.
5. The Editor's decision is final. No correspondence can be entered into, and entries cannot be returned.

20 Runners-up prizes of a complete set of Cub Scout Activity and Puzzle Books

Competition

1 TURKEY

2

3

4 Sweden

5 Canada

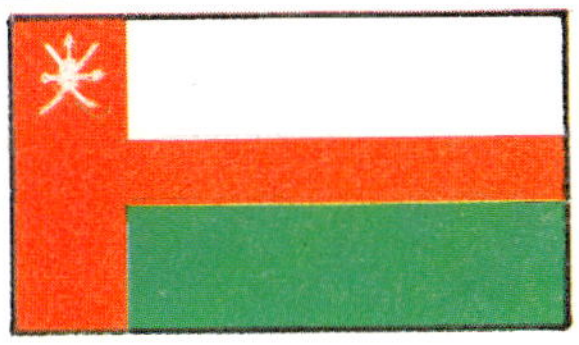

6

7 United King

8

9

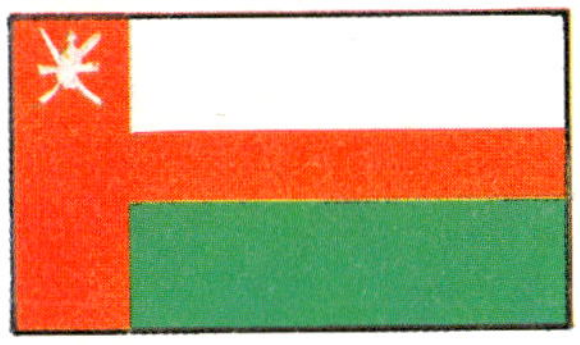

10

11

12

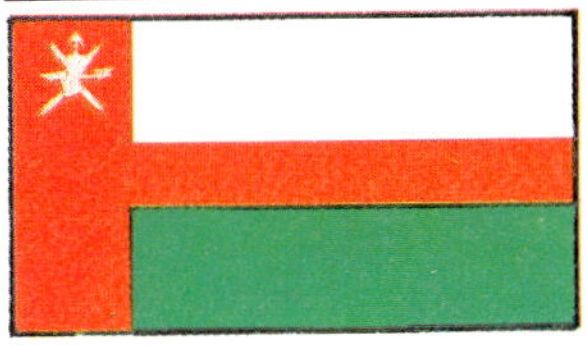

13

14 Italy

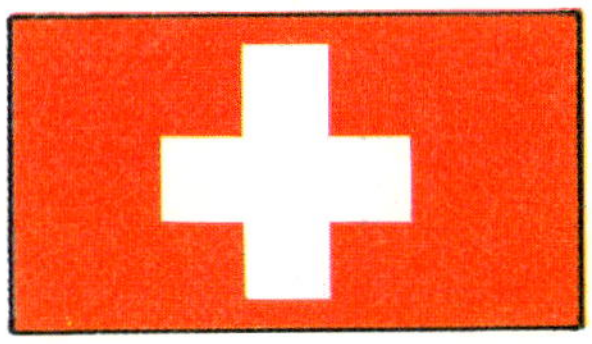

15 Swetzerland

Now put your correct answers on the entry form on page 61.

You will find all the flags illustrated here in *The International Cub Scout Book*, or in books about flags in your school or local public library.

year's competition is sponsored by

Sinclair Research Ltd

sinclair

and

World International Publishing Ltd

World

A SCIENCE CROSSWORD

by Niva Miles

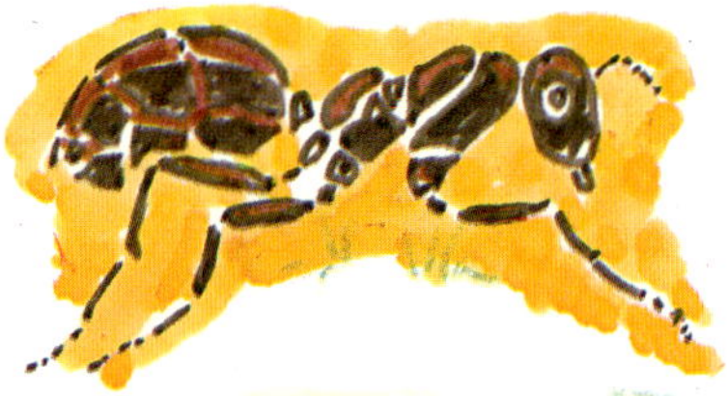

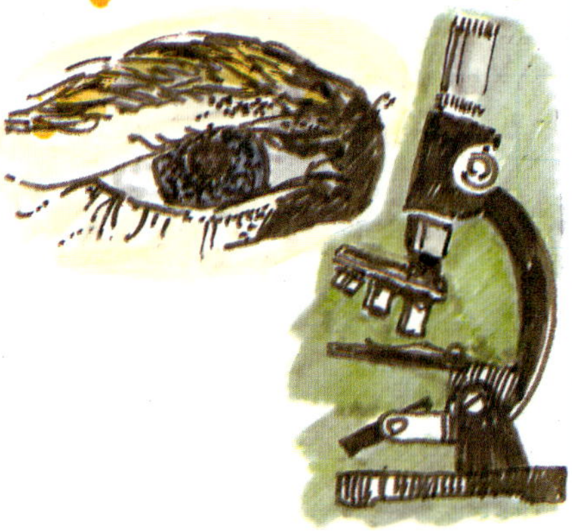

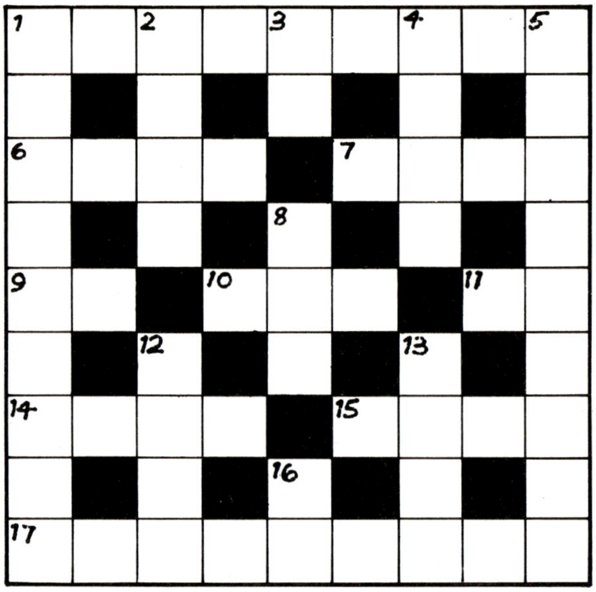

CLUES ACROSS

1. A sheet of muscle below your chest (9)
6. Causes disease (4)
7. A broad one could never be a runner (4)
9. Antimony (symbol) (2)
10. From olives, or the North Sea (3)
11. π? (2)
14. A flower in the eye (4)
15. Remove the dog from curtail (4)
17. False ones make the lids heavy (9)

CLUES DOWN

1. A biscuit eaten by a body system (9)
2. 4,840 square yards (4)
3. Helium (symbol) (2)
4. Latin name for birds (4)
5. Jaws (9)
8. A metal can (3)
12. It flies when you are having fun (4)
13. Spotty — a skinful! (4)
16. Sodium (symbol) (2)

Solution on page 63

Find the Proficiency Badges

by Suzanne Brown

There are no clues to this puzzleword! All you have to do is to fill in the blank squares to make the names of ten of the Cub Scout Proficiency Badges.

Solution on page 63

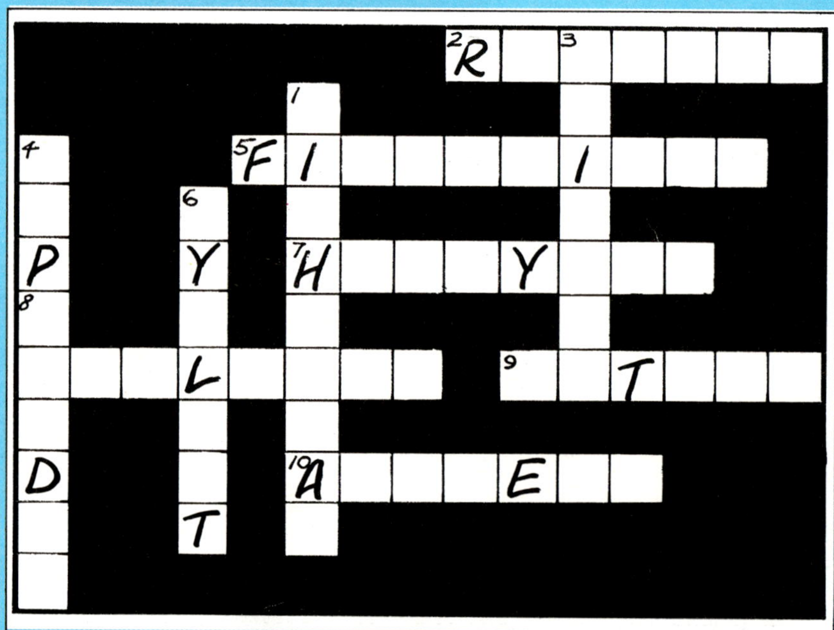

Name the Flags Competition

Entry Form

closing date
31st January 1986

Special Notes

1. Full details of the Competition are given on pages 58 and 59.
2. If you do not wish to cut out this page from your Annual, you may photocopy it for your Competition Entry.
3. The 1986 Cub Scout Annual Challenge is on the next page so if you want to have a go at the Challenge, make sure you do so before sending off this form.

To: 1986 CUB SCOUT ANNUAL COMPETITION
Editorial Department, The Scout Association,
Baden-Powell House, Queen's Gate,
LONDON, SW7 5JS

PLEASE COMPLETE THIS FORM IN BLOCK CAPITALS

NAME ______________________

ADDRESS ______________________

____

____

____

CUB SCOUT PACK ______________________

____

DATE OF BIRTH ______________________

Please complete this section as well:
The three items I most enjoyed in this Annual were:

1. ______________________
2. ______________________
3. ______________________

I would like to make these suggestions for features in future Cub Scout Annuals:

1. ______________________
2. ______________________
3. ______________________

Name the Flag Competition		Answers
Flag No.	Name of Country (BLOCK CAPITALS)	
1	T	U R K E Y
2		
3		
4		
5		
6		
7		
8		
9		
10		
11		
12		
13		
14		
15		

Now take the first letter of each answer and put them in the boxes below.

1	2	3	4	5	6	7	8
T							

9	10	11	12	13	14	15

Complete the sentence here:

____

____

In the 1984 CUB SCOUT ANNUAL we asked readers to draw what they thought was 'A Typical Cub Scout'. We had lots of entries, and you can see those which we chose for publication on pages 14 and 15 of this year's Annual.

Now for this year's Challenge!

I'M A CUB SCOUT BECAUSE . . .

Around the world there are hundreds of thousands of boys who are Cub Scouts. You are one of those boys. You are a Cub Scout because . . . Hey! Wait a minute. Do you want *us* to tell *you* why you are a Cub? Probably not, because you are able to speak for yourself. And that's just what we'd like you to do. *You* tell *us* why you're a Cub Scout.

Starting with the phrase 'I'm a Cub Scout because . . .' give us your reason (or reasons) for being a Cub in not more than 30 words. Send your entry on a POSTCARD (and don't forget your name, address and Cub Scout Pack) to arrive not later than 31st January 1986 to:

Cub Scout Annual
Editorial Department
The Scout Association
Baden-Powell House
Queen's Gate
LONDON SW7 5JS

The writer of each entry selected for publication will receive a FREE copy of the 1988 CUB SCOUT ANNUAL. (Yes, we do mean the 1988 CUB SCOUT ANNUAL because your Annual has to be prepared almost a year before you can buy it in the shops. By the time you read this, the 1987 Annual will be almost complete.)